THE LITURGY
OF
CHRISTIAN BURIAL

ALCUIN CLUB COLLECTIONS
No. 59

THE LITURGY

OF

CHRISTIAN BURIAL

*An Introductory Survey
of the Historical Development of
Christian Burial Rites*

by
GEOFFREY ROWELL

ALCUIN CLUB/S.P.C.K.

First published in 1977
for the Alcuin Club
by S.P.C.K.
Holy Trinity Church
Marylebone Road
London NW1 4DU

Printed in Great Britain by William Clowes & Sons, Limited
London, Beccles and Colchester

ISBN 0 281 03579 2

In memoriam matrinae meae dilectissimae
Margaretta Hunter
(1898–1963)
In paradisum deducant te angeli

Contents

Preface

Considering that death is one of the most significant moments of human experience, and that a funeral, even in our secular society, is one of the major occasions when even those who have little contact with the Church participate in Christian worship, it is surprising that there appears to be no study of the history of the liturgy of Christian burial. This short introductory survey has been written in the hope that it will not only do something to fill this gap, but, by showing something of the different ways in which Christians have expressed their understanding of death and burial, may also be of use to those concerned to find appropriate words and symbols for Christian funeral liturgy today.

The genesis of this book was an essay on the subject of the liturgy of Christian burial, for which I was awarded the George Williams Prize at Cambridge in 1965. The late Professor E. C. Ratcliff, the examiner, from whose lectures on other aspects of liturgy I had greatly profited, encouraged me to consider writing a fuller account of the liturgy of burial. The present work would not, I fear, satisfy his rigorous standards, or count as the exhaustive treatment he suggested I should write, but I hope that he would have thought it worthwhile within its self-chosen limitations. I am grateful for his advice and comment many years ago, and for help given by others, in particular Mr C. M. Smith and Dr S. P. Brock. I would also like to thank Mrs E. Ackroyd, who in typing the manuscript was inevitably confronted with a perpetual *memento mori*.

Keble College, Oxford. GEOFFREY ROWELL
Advent, 1976.

I *Jewish and pagan influence on Christian practice*

All rites and ceremonies concerned with the three significant moments of human life—birth, marriage, and death—are conservative in character. The actions and words with which men surround these momentous occasions become fixed, as expressions of the judgments made about human life and its meaning, and as points by which men may re-orientate themselves in known and familiar ways to new situations. New world-views may lead to new interpretations and to the compiling of new rites and ceremonies, but alongside these new forms the old customs tend to survive, though they are frequently given a new rationale.

The burial rites and customs of the Christian church are no exception to this general pattern. Not only do we find in them the traces of Jewish practice which we would expect, but also a number of survivals from pagan worship, particularly in the case of unofficial folk-customs and ceremonies.

The evidence for the early centuries is, unfortunately, scanty. Christians inherited from Judaism the practice of burial as the accepted method of disposal of the dead. Burials and burial customs were, therefore, not anything new as far as Christians were concerned. Neither were they a primary focus of Christian worship, with the possible exception of the developed martyr-cult. Even here attention was concentrated on the tomb as a place of veneration after burial, rather than the burial itself. Because of this strong element of continuity, such references as we have to the early development of Christian burial rites and ceremonies are largely derived from occasional comments in works whose main interest lies elsewhere, and this means that our knowledge is inevitably fragmentary.

The pattern of burial customs is basically dictated by the

practical necessity of disposing of the body of the dead man as reverently and as efficiently as possible. In hot climates, in which the body quickly begins to decay and becomes a danger to health, this means that burial must follow very soon after death. Again, the location of burial grounds outside towns, for reasons of health and because the presence of a dead body was regarded as polluting, meant that the funeral procession from the place of death to the burial ground became an important feature of the liturgy of burial.

In the absence of any evidence to the contrary, it must be supposed that Christian practice began by following that of Judaism, with customs derived from pagan practice exerting an increasing influence as the proportion of Gentile Christians increased. In particular, the New Testament accounts of the burial of Jesus are likely to have provided a norm for Christian burial, though the details given in the gospels are in fact few enough. First there is the simple point that Jesus was buried in accordance with Jewish custom. The Synoptic Gospels then speak of his body being wrapped in a linen cloth (σινδών), though there is not the usual anointing of the body at this stage, presumably because of the special circumstances, the sabbath and the very natural fear of the authorities. Luke mentions the preparation of spices and myrrh (ἀρώματα καὶ μύρα) just before the sabbath begins, and Mark and Luke make the bringing of these materials to the tomb the occasion of the women's visit to it on the Sunday morning. The Fourth Gospel has a different account. The body is wrapped in linen bands (ὀθόνια), with the spices, described as myrrh and aloes, placed in between the strips as was customary.[1] In the account of the empty tomb a further detail is mentioned—the σουδάριον which was round his head. The same term is used to describe part of the grave-clothes of Lazarus, though in the case of Lazarus the word κειρία and not ὀθόνια is used for the material with which the body is bound.[2] *Mishnah Shabbath* xxiii.5 permits the binding of the chin of a corpse on the sabbath day, and it is probably the material used for this purpose to which the word σουδάριον refers.

Other accounts of burial in the New Testament give us little comparative data. In Acts Ananias is said to be carried out by the young men who συνέστειλαν αὐτόν, but in the context this can hardly be a reference to grave-clothes, and probably refers to his cloak, especially as there is no mention of any wrapping of the body in the case of Sapphira.[3] Stephen, we are merely told, was buried καὶ ἐποίησαν κοπετὸν μέγαν ἐπ᾽ αὐτῷ. In the case of Tabitha of Joppa a further detail is added, namely the washing of the body, and it is possible that the weeping widows mentioned later in the story are professional mourners, as well as being the recipients of Tabitha's charity.[4] In Luke's account of the raising of the widow's son at Nain a considerable crowd is mentioned as forming the funeral procession to the place of burial.[5]

Jewish Traditions

The Jewish liturgy of burial, the *Tzidduk Ha-din*, or 'Justification of Judgment', dates as a written text from the ninth century, when the Gaonim, the 'grand rabbis' of Babylonia, issued orders of prayers for the guidance of distant congregations. There are, however, elements in the liturgy, which can be traced back through the Talmud and Mishnah to an earlier date, and the Talmud and Mishnah themselves provide numerous regulations for burial and for mourning, though the precise dating of some of these is difficult to ascertain. The very existence of these regulations makes it clear that the burial of the dead was one of the important religious obligations in Judaism.[6] Dead bodies were regarded as unclean, and therefore had to be disposed of in the proper way before a man was permitted to engage once more in his regular religious duties. *Mishnah Berakoth* iii.1, for example, forbids a man with an unburied corpse in his house to recite the *Shema* and to wear phylacteries. The same prohibition applies to the bearers, and to all who assist in any material way at the funeral. In the Talmud we find a considerable list of things forbidden to a mourner.

> He is forbidden to do work, to bathe, or anoint himself, to have (marital) intercourse, or don sandals; he is forbidden to read the Pentateuch, Prophets, or Hagiographa, or to recite the Mishnah, or Midrash and *halacoth*, or the Talmud or *aggadoth*. If, however, the public have need of him, he need not abstain.[7]

The mourner was also exempt from certain of the sabbath regulations. *Mishnah Shabbath* xxiii.4, 5 permits the preparation of all that is needful for the dead, and the anointing and washing of the body on the sabbath, providing only that the position of the limbs remains undisturbed. Similarly a mattress may be removed from underneath the body, in order that it may be laid on sand

3

and so be better preserved until the funeral. The Talmudic tractate on mourning, ironically called *Semaḥoth*, 'joys', gives elaborate mourning rituals, some of which are thought to go back to R. Eliezer b. Zadok, and to reflect the practice in Palestine in the first century A.D.

In its developed pattern mourning fell into three periods; three 'days of weeping'; a period up to the seventh day, with abstention from work and any personal care and adornment; and finally a period of slightly mitigated formal mourning down to the thirtieth day. There appear to be references to the first two periods in Ecclesiasticus.

> Weep bitterly, wail most fervently; observe the mourning the dead man deserves, one day, or two, to avoid comment, and then be comforted in your sorrow. Mourning for the dead lasts seven days, and for the foolish and ungodly all the days of their lives.[8]

The seven days mourning period was frequently justified from the time of Joseph's mourning for Jacob, and the thirty days period from the time of mourning for Moses according to Deuteronomy xxxiv.8.[9]

According to *Semaḥoth* it was the custom to erect wedding canopies at the funerals of couples who had died before their marriage. At royal funerals it was permitted to burn articles, though many of the rabbis disapproved of this practice because of the waste involved. A key and writing-tablet were sometimes suspended from the coffin of a dead man.[10] Funeral processions were required to give way to bridal processions, on the grounds that death must give way to life.[11] After the funeral a meal was provided for the male, but not apparently for the female mourners. This meal was known as the *labra'ah*, or 'meal of comfort'. It was prepared by friends, and consisted of lentils and eggs, the round shape of which was supposedly a reminder of the revolving wheel of fortune.[12] Two cups of wine were drunk before the meal, five during it, and three after it; 'namely for the benediction of mourners, one for the consolation of mourners, and one (in honour of) charity'.[13] Three further cups were added later, for the synagogue, and in memory of Rabbi Gamaliel.

Gamaliel II (A.D. 80–120) was head of the rabbinical academy at Yavneh, and was particularly remembered as the man largely responsible for reducing the cost of funerals. Before his time, these had often involved inordinate expense, and Josephus notes that the necessity of providing funeral feasts for the populace had impoverished many Jews.[14] The opposition of some rabbis to the expensive habit of burying large numbers of garments with the body is mentioned in *Semaḥoth*.[15] The tractate *Mo'ed Katan* indicates how funeral practice was modified in order to reduce ostentation and social division.

> Our Rabbis taught: Formerly they were wont to convey (victuals) to the house of mourning, the rich in silver and gold baskets, and the poor in osier baskets of peeled willow twigs, and the poor felt shamed; they therefore instituted that all should convey (victuals) in osier baskets of peeled willow twigs out of deference to the poor.
>
> Our Rabbis taught: Formerly they were wont to serve drinks in a house of mourning, the rich in white glass vessels, and the poor in coloured glass, and the poor felt shamed; they instituted therefore that all should serve drinks in coloured glass, out of deference to the poor. Formerly they were wont to uncover the face of the rich and to cover the face of the poor, because their faces turned livid in years of drought, and the poor felt shamed; they therefore instituted that everyone's face should be covered out of deference for the poor. Formerly they were wont to bring out the rich (for burial) on a *dargesh* (tall state bed, ornamented and covered with rich coverlets) and the poor on a plain bier, and the poor felt shamed; they instituted therefore that all should be brought out on a plain bier, out of deference to the poor . . .
>
> Formerly the (expense of) taking the dead out (to his burial) fell harder on his near-of-kin than his death, so that the dead man's near-of-kin abandoned him and fled, until at last Rabban Gamaliel came (forward) and disregarding his own dignity, came out (to his burial) in flaxen vestments. Said R. Papa, And nowadays all the world follow the practice of (coming out) even in a paltry (shroud) that costs but a *zuz*.[16]

When death occurred in a house all couches were to be overturned. This, it has been suggested, was to serve as a symbolic warning against sexual intercourse, which was prohibited during the days of mourning.[17] Again, all water in the house was to be thrown away as unclean. This was based on the ruling of Numbers xix.15, which declared that all open vessels in a tent where death had occurred were to be regarded as unclean until seven days after the death. Many explanations have been advanced for this. It may have been thought that the soul cleansed itself in water after death, and it would therefore be dangerous for the living to use; or that the angel of death cleansed his sword in it; or simply that water represented life, and hence had no place in a house in which death had occurred.[18]

The arrangements for funerals were generally made by local burial societies (*chevra kaddisha*), which collected funds for the purpose from all who had resided in the locality for more than nine months.[19] On the return from the burial ground there was an elaborate ritual of comforting the mourners to be observed. According to *Baba Bathra* 100b there were seven halts on the return from the burial ground, and at each of these everyone in the funeral procession sat down and offered consolation to the mourners. It seems to have been the practice in Judaea, according to R. Judah, for the leader to call out after each offering of consolation 'Stand, dear (friends), stand up', and then, after walking some distance to call out again, 'Sit down, dear (friends), sit down'.[20]

As we have already noticed, there was no written liturgy of burial until some time in the ninth century A.D. Indeed, it was not until that time that there were any written prayers at all, the living oral tradition being highly valued, so that, as *Shabbath* 115b put it, 'those who write down benedictions are like unto them who burn the Torah'. There is an early reference, however, to mourners tearing their upper garments about three inches, and saying, as the body was lowered into the grave, 'Blessed be the Judge of Truth'.[21] Of the Jewish burial liturgy as we now have it, one element is certainly very ancient. That is the *Kaddish*. This was the prayer with which the normal synagogue liturgy ended, and it is echoed in the beginning of the Lord's Prayer. In its earliest established form it ran as follows:

> Exalted and hallowed be his great name
>   in the world which he created according to his will.
> May he let his kingdom rule
>   in your lifetime and in your days and in the lifetime
>   of the whole house of Israel, speedily and soon.
> Praised be his great name from eternity to eternity.
>   And to this say: Amen.[22]

In the form in which it became incorporated into the accepted funeral liturgy it contained an extra, special petition, praying that God would 'revive the dead, and raise them up to life eternal'. In its original form and context it was an eschatological prayer, looking for the establishment of God's rule and kingdom, and as such could easily come to have a special reference to the individual's hope of resurrection at the time of God's Messianic intervention, and so be appropriately used as part of the liturgy of burial. Idelsohn notes a legend of Akiba teaching an orphan to say the *Kaddish* in order to save his father from Gehenna, and this theme was elaborated in later *midrashim*.[23]

The *Tzidduk Ha-din*, as it is now found in the Authorized Jewish Prayer Book, begins with an affirmation of the justice and righteousness of God in all his actions, in death and judgment as well as in life. The first words are taken from Deuteronomy xxxii.4: 'The Rock, his work is perfect, for all his ways are judgment: a God of faithfulness and without iniquity, just and right is he.' There follow a number of verses extolling the perfection of God in his words and deeds, and praying also that he will show mercy and compassion to the mourners and to those who are still alive. This section concludes with verses taken from the Psalms, Jeremiah, and Job.

Thou art great in counsel and mighty in deed; thine eyes are open upon all ways of the children of men, to give unto everyone according to the fruit of his doing. To declare that the Lord is upright; he is my Rock, and there is no unfaithfulness in him.

The Lord gave, and the Lord hath taken away: blessed be the Name of the Lord. And he being merciful, forgiveth iniquity and destroyeth not: yea many a time he turneth his anger away, and doth stir up all his wrath.[24]

Then follows Psalm xvi, with its reference to God not abandoning the soul to Sheol, and showing to man the path of life, bringing him to the joy of his presence. The coffin is then taken to the burial ground. At the burial ground those who have not visited it for thirty days are instructed to say a prayer in which they affirm the justice of God, and praise him as the one who revives the dead.

Blessed be the Lord our God, King of the universe, who formed you in judgment, who nourished and sustained you in judgment, who brought death on you in judgment, who knoweth the number of you all in judgment, and will hereafter restore you to life in judgment. Blessed art thou, O Lord, who revivest the dead.

Thou, O Lord, art mighty for ever, thou revivest the dead, thou art mighty to save.

Thou sustainest the falling, healest the sick, loosest the bound, and keepest thy faith to them that sleep in the dust: who is like unto thee, Lord of mighty acts, and who resembleth thee, O King, who orderest death and restorest life, and causest salvation to spring forth? Yea, faithful art thou to revive the dead.

The coffin is then lowered into the grave with the words, 'May he (she) come to his (her) place in peace'. As the mourners leave the burial ground it is customary for them to pluck some grass, repeating the words from Isaiah xxvi.19, 'And they of the city shall flourish like the grass of the earth', and Psalm ciii.14, 'He remembereth that we are but dust'. All who are present at the burial are required to wash their hands, saying as they do so, 'He maketh death to vanish in life eternal; and the Lord God wipeth away tears from all faces; and the reproach of his people shall he take away from the earth; for the Lord hath spoken it' (Isaiah xxv.8), and on returning to the synagogue hall Psalm xc.17 is recited: 'May the graciousness of the Lord our God be upon us'. At the burial of their parents children are required to say the funeral *Kaddish*, to which the congregation replies, 'Let his great name be blessed for ever and to all eternity'. The mourners and the congregation then say together:

> Blessed, praised and glorified, exalted, extolled, honoured, magnified and lauded be the Name of the Holy One, blessed be he; though he be high above all blessing and hymns, praises and consolations, which are uttered in the world; and say ye, Amen.
>
> May there be abundant peace from heaven, and life for us and for all Israel; and say ye, Amen.
>
> He maketh peace in his high places, may he work peace for us and for all Israel; and say ye, Amen.[25]

This liturgy of the *Tzidduk Ha-din* is a very late development, and we must not look for textual influence on Christian rites. Nevertheless, its stark simplicity and directness, and its consciousness of the righteous justice and faithfulness of God, who is to be praised in death as well as in life, exemplify the Jewish response to suffering and death, which is the context out of which the Christian understanding developed. Its very simplicity points us to a basic pattern of strongly biblical prayer, accompanying the few necessary actions of burial, which may be assumed, with the necessary Christological additions, to reflect what is most likely to have been the earliest Christian practice.

Pagan Influences

Pagan practice undoubtedly influenced the development of Christian funerary rites and ceremonies at a number of points, and there are references in the Fathers to attempts to control popular customs which were regarded as improper for Christians to follow. The burial rites and customs of the Graeco-Roman world were naturally varied, but Roman practice was in the first Christian centuries the most influential. Cremation, which had been the dominant Roman way of disposing of the dead was, by the second century, rapidly giving way to burial, though this does not seem to have been the result of Jewish or Christian influence, but rather reflects, as Professor Toynbee has pointed out, 'a significant strengthening of emphasis on the individual's enjoyment of a blissful hereafter'.[26]

Toynbee gives a clear account of the *funus translaticum*, the normal funeral ritual, which was followed in the burial of ordinary citizens.[27] On the approach of death the relatives and friends of the dying man gathered around his bed, and, as he drew his last breath, his nearest relative gave the last kiss, so as to catch the soul which was breathed out. Then the eyes of the departed were closed (*oculos premere*), and near relatives called on the dead man by name and bewailed his passing. The body was then placed on the ground (*deponere*), was washed and anointed, and, if the deceased was a male, the body was dressed in a toga and a wreath was placed on the head. A coin was placed in the dead man's mouth to serve as Charon's fee for ferrying the departed soul across the Styx to the abode of the dead. This custom, perhaps first developed as a symbolic substitute for the earlier practice of burying a quantity of the dead man's possessions with him, was taken over by the Romans from the Greeks.[28] When the preparation of the body was completed, it was replaced on the bed, with the feet turned towards the door of the house, where it lay in state until the time of the funeral procession. This funeral procession, the following of the corpse to burial, was an important part of Roman burial practice, as it was in Jewish, and from it derive the terms *exsequiae* and *prosequi* to describe the funeral and those attending it. Black garments (*lugubria*) were worn by those taking part in the funeral procession.

The bier was carried by four to eight bearers, with the body lying on a funerary couch. Musicians might precede it in the procession. If the dead man was distinguished, the body would be placed on the rostra in the Forum and an encomium would be pronounced. It was customary for masks of the dead man's ancestors to be preserved, and these would be worn by other members of his family in the funeral procession. If the body was to be cremated, the eyes of the corpse were re-opened when it was placed on the funerary fire. After the cremation was over, the ashes would be drenched with wine.

On returning from the funeral all the relatives of the departed had to undergo the *suffitio*, a rite of purification by fire and water, and there would also be cleansing ceremonies (*feriae denicales*) at the house of the deceased. Later, the funeral feast, the *silicernium*, would take place at the grave of the dead, and a further feast, at which a libation to the *manes* was poured on to the burial, was held on the ninth day after the funeral (*cena novem-dialis*) to mark the end of the period of full mourning.

Of these pagan customs the most important of those which came to be associated with Christian rites for the dead in the early centuries were probably the ones connected with the various funeral feasts, and the days of commemoration after the actual burial. Jewish practice, as we have seen, included a funeral feast, but in Judaism this took place in the house, and not at the graveside, as was the Roman custom. In Roman religion the funeral feast was clearly connected with the belief that the dead required nourishment in some way, and that the tedium of their existence in the tomb could be relieved by participation in a feast held by their relatives and friends at their place of burial. There are a number of Roman tombs in existence with holes in their outer coverings to permit libations to be poured on to the corpse or ashes of the dead, and other tombs which consist, not only of a burial chamber, but also of a dining-room (*triclinium*) and sometimes a kitchen.[29] These graveside funeral feasts were often riotous and drunken occasions, and the church disliked them both for this reason and because of their implications concerning the state of the departed. Tertullian saw no difference between funeral feasts and feasts of Jupiter, and described those who took part in them as making an offering to themselves rather than to the departed and returning drunk from the feasts.[30] In the late fourth century the author of the *Apostolic Constitutions* warns Christians against the same excesses when they are invited to pagan funeral feasts.

> Now when you are invited to their memorials, do you feast with good order, and the fear of God, as disposed to intercede for those that are departed. For since you are presbyters and deacons of Christ, you ought always to be sober, both among yourselves and among others, that so you may be able to warn the unruly . . . We say this, not that they are not to drink at all, otherwise it would be to the reproach of

what God has made for cheerfulness, but that they be not disordered
with wine . . . Nor do we say this only to those of the clergy, but also
to every lay Christian, upon whom the name of our Lord Jesus Christ
is called.[31]

These funeral feasts were private family commemorations and
as such difficult for the clergy effectively to control. The same
difficulty arose in the extension of the practice in a more public
way with the growth of the martyr-cult in North Africa in
particular. The annual commemoration of the martyr's death
had the character of merely being a more solemn form of the
private funeral feast, the *refrigerium* or 'refreshment', as it was
known. The general way in which the church attempted to
control the practice was by the substitution of a funeral eucharist
for the pagan rites, and by an insistence on the funeral feast being
used to provide food for the poor, not an excuse for indulgence for
the living with overtones of the food being in some way beneficial
to the dead. In Milan Ambrose took a stricter attitude,
forbidding the *refrigerium* altogether. Augustine records in the
Confessions how, when his mother Monnica, used to the customs of
the African church, 'brought to the churches built in memory of
the saints, certain cakes, and bread and wine', she was forbidden
to do so by the door-keeper, carrying out the bishop's orders.
Augustine describes his mother's accustomed practice in detail.

When she had brought her basket with the accustomed festival-food,
to be but tasted by herself, and then given away, [she] never joined
therewith more than one small cup of wine, diluted according to her
own abstemious habits, which for courtesy she would taste. And if
there were many churches of the departed saints, that were to be
honoured in that manner, she still carried round that same one cup,
to be used everywhere; and this, though not only made very watery,
but unpleasantly heated with carrying about, she would distribute to
those about her by small sips; for she sought their devotion, not
pleasure.[32]

Augustine attempted later to regulate the practice of the African
Church, not by an absolute ban on the *refrigerium* such as
Ambrose imposed, but by requiring that only moderate gifts
should be offered at the tombs of the dead, and by emphasizing
that the 'refreshment' consisted in the relief afforded to the poor
by their receipt of the gifts.[33] In the *Enchiridion* he argued that the
souls of the dead, which until the final resurrection were kept in a
hidden retreat, enjoying rest or suffering hardship in accordance

with what they merited during their life in the body, were helped by the piety of the living, the eucharistic sacrifice and almsgiving. Those only profit, however, 'who, when alive, earned merit so such things could profit them'.[34] The *Apostolic Constitutions* likewise urge that alms should be given to the poor from the property of a departed Christian.[35]

Closely associated with the practice of funeral meals were the commemoration days themselves. In Greece, and the eastern Mediterranean generally, the main funeral feast had always been associated with the third day after burial rather than being held, like the Roman *silicernium*, on the day of burial itself.[36] As a consequence the observance of a commemoration on the third day became almost universal, particularly as it coincided with the end of the 'days of weeping', the first period of Jewish mourning. The ninth and fortieth days after death were also observed as days of commemoration. Various suggestions have been made concerning the origin of the fortieth day. Jungmann argues that it is likely to be connected with primitive theories about the birth of the individual, the fortieth day being that on which it was believed that the embryo took the form of a child and received a soul.[37] Cumont, on the other hand, prefers an astrological explanation:

> The Syrians, at the critical times in which the moonbeams exercised a more active influence on this separation (of soul and body through the corrupting action of moonbeams on the flesh), offered sacrifices on the tombs, and the threefold commemoration of the dead on the third, the seventh, and the fortieth day in a part of the Eastern Church had its earliest origin in these offerings of the sidereal cults.[38]

When these pagan commemoration days passed into Christian observance, they were, of course, given an explanation in Christian terms. The third day was clearly justified by the Resurrection of Christ on the third day, and, where the seventh day was observed, which again was the Jewish custom, the Genesis creation narrative provided a basis for the practice. The fortieth was more difficult. The *Apostolic Constitutions* cite the mourning for Moses as the justification, but the relevant text in Deuteronomy in fact refers to thirty days, which some manuscripts give as an alternative reading.[39] The justification from Deuteronomy is certainly later than the practice of observing the fortieth day, and probably originally belonged to the Jewish basis for keeping the thirtieth day.[40] There would seem, in fact, to have been two traditions current in Palestine, for evidence for observance of the fortieth day can be found in the writings of Damascene[41] and Chrysostom,[42] and can be traced back as early as Philo[43] and the book of *Jubilees*.[44] The ninth day celebrated by the Greek Church is justified by Photius on the ground of the Lord's appearance to Thomas 'after eight days', and he refers to the Ascension as the explanation for the fortieth day. Freistedt suggests, however, that a truer explanation of the fortieth day is to be found in the end of mourning in a variant Jewish tradition, and cites the Slavonic *Book of Adam* as evidence of the existence of a 7–9–40 schema. In this work Michael is represented as telling Seth to 'arrange the memorial feasts on the third day and the ninth and on the twentieth and on the fortieth'. No explanation is offered for the inclusion of the twentieth day, which is not found in any of the major Christian commemoration orders.[45] These local variations emerged from the combination of Jewish and pagan practice and differed mainly as to whether the second commemoration day was the seventh or the ninth, and the third commemoration the thirtieth or the fortieth. Freistedt has shown in detail the different local patterns.[46]

A. Eastern Church

Greek	Armenian	Syrian		Egyptian		Palestine
		(Greek)	(National)	(Greek)	(National)	
3	3	3	3	3	3	3
9	9 or ?7	9 and 15	?9	9 and 12	9	7
40	40	40	30	40 and 14	?30	40

B. Western Church

City of Rome	Gaul	Gothic	Milanese	Mozarabic	African
3	3	3	—	—	3
7 and ?9	7	7 and 9	7	—	7 and (?9)
30	30	30	40	?50	—

Another point at which pagan practice influenced Christian custom was in the viaticum. As Grabka has shown,[47] the cultural background of the viaticum is one of considerable complexity. The natural desire to aid the dead, in whatever state of existence they were, was reflected in the various funeral meals and sacrifices held at tombs. There was also a general belief that, after death, men embarked on a voyage to their final resting-place, however that was conceived. Such a voyage was likely to be fraught with peril, and it was necessary to have both a guide and provisions for the journey. As we have seen, it was the usual Greek and Roman practice to bury the dead with a coin in their mouth, which was interpreted as Charon's fee—necessary in order that the soul should reach the end of its journey in safety. In Latin this coin was sometimes described as *viaticum*, though this originally had the more extended meaning of the food, supplies, and funds collected together for a journey. In Christian usage *viaticum*, and its Greek equivalent ἐφόδιον, was often used as a description of those things which guarded and preserved a Christian throughout his life, such as his baptism, faith, monastic life, or good works.[48] This was particularly referred to the eucharist, and especially to the communion which came to be given immediately before death. As early as the first *Apology* of Justin there is reference to the giving of communion to the sick,[49] and by the time of the council of Nicaea the practice of giving communion to the dying as their *viaticum* seems to have been regarded as an ancient and long-standing tradition.[50] Eusebius records a story, apparently deriving from Dionysius of Alexandria, of the miraculous preservation of a dying man, Serapion, until he had received the eucharist,[51] and there are examples of Christians wishing to die with the eucharist in their mouths, and for it to be buried with them, in much the same manner as the old coin for Charon. The apocryphal life of St Basil depicts Basil as dying 'with the eucharist still in his mouth', and the life of St Melania states that it is the Roman custom that 'when souls depart the communion of the Lord should be in the mouth'.[52] Paulinus in his account of the death of Ambrose speaks of Ambrose being offered 'the Body of the Lord, which he received, and as soon as he had swallowed it, he breathed forth his spirit, bearing with him a good viaticum, so that his soul, more refreshed by this food, now rejoices in the company of angels, according to whose life he lived on earth'.[53] The *Statuta Ecclesiae Antiqua*, which probably date from the late fifth century and are of Gallican provenance, provide that, if a dying man lingers on for some time before death comes, the eucharist should be placed in his mouth.[54] The giving of communion to the dead, and the burial of the dead with the eucharist in their mouths, were frequently condemned by the councils of the church. The council of Hippo in 393 has a canon prohibiting the giving of the eucharist to the bodies of the dead, and the council of Carthage in 419 followed the same line. 'It also seemed good that the eucharist should not be given to the bodies of the dead. For it is written "Take, eat," but the bodies of the dead can neither "take" nor "eat"'.[55] Chrysostom had used a similar argument, when he had asked whether Christ spoke of the living or the dead when he said 'Except you eat . . . you have no life'.[56] There are further condemnations of the practice at Carthage (525), Auxerre (578), and at the council in Trullo (692). The council of Auxerre also condemned the practice of giving the last kiss to the dead, probably because of its association with pagan beliefs about catching the soul of the dying man and so preserving it in the family.[57]

It is not surprising that, under the influence of pagan customs, some Christians should have treated the eucharist as the equivalent of Charon's fee, but this was not the only justification of the viaticum. There was a long tradition of theology going back to Ignatius of Antioch which spoke of the eucharist as the 'medicine of immortality' and 'the antidote against death'.[58] Irenaeus referred to the eucharist as bestowing incorruptibility upon men's bodies,[59] and Gregory of Nyssa wrote, that 'just as a little bit of leaven, as the Apostle says, changes all of the dough into itself, so too that body which was brought to death by God, once it enters into us, transforms and changes all into itself'.[60] A ritual of the seventh century goes as far as to make the viaticum the operative agent of the resurrection: 'the communion will be to him a protection and an aid in the resurrection for the just, for it will itself raise him again'.[61]

The liturgical formulae for the administration of the viaticum, and the concluding prayers were not fixed until the thirteenth century, when various Carolingian forms were adopted. Until the twelfth century it was common for the viaticum to be given either by taking the sick person to church for the eucharist, or by having a celebration of the eucharist in the house. For a long time the Lord's Prayer was prescribed as the principal preparation for communion, but at the end of the eleventh century this was replaced by the *Confiteor* and the giving of a proof of faith.[62]

The viaticum tradition was, as we have seen, closely linked with the imagery of death as a journey, and a journey beset with perils. In many later prayers we find a flowing together of the idea of the voyage of death with the theme of the ship of the church traversing the perilous seas to arrive at the haven which is heaven.[63] Or the emphasis could fall on the dangers of the journey, represented dramatically by malevolent lions and dragons. In I Peter v.8 the devil is referred to as a roaring lion prowling after his prey, and lions are one of the dangers of the wilderness through which the people of God must pass on their exodus, so that the absence or obedience of lions and other wild beasts is one of the characteristics of the new paradise which God will establish.[64] This understanding of the lion as one of the dangers of the wilderness passed over into later Jewish and Christian imagery of hell. The *Torath Adam* says of hell, that

> in it are many caverns, and in them are fiery lions, and when a man falls into one of these caverns the lions devour him, and when he is consumed he appears again as perfect as if he had not been touched by fire, and then they who are thus restored thrown again into the fire of every cavern.[65]

A couplet of Peter Damian's *De Poenis Infernis Rhythmus* provides a good example from medieval Christian hymnody:

> adsunt fremitus leonum, sibili serpentium,
> quibus mixti confunduntur ululatus flentium.[66]

In the offertory sentence of the Roman requiem mass there is a petition that the souls of the departed may be 'delivered from the mouth of the lion, that hell may not swallow them up and that they may not fall into darkness'.

If death is a journey beset by dangers, then there is need of a guide through these dangers. In classical mythology the gods are often represented as acting as escorts for the souls of the dead, and Hermes is frequently found as the one who brings souls from this world to Charon's ferry. In Judaism the angels came to be thought of as the guides of the dead. The Old Testament represents angels as guiding men during life, and it is not therefore surprising that, as a doctrine of a future life was elaborated, they should come to have the same function there also.[67] The *Testament of Asher* contrasts the soul of the unrighteous man, which at death is tormented by the evil spirit which it served in life, with that of the man at peace with God, who 'goes to meet the angel of peace, who leads him to eternal life'.[68] As Daniélou has pointed out, this is a development from early apocalyptic, in which angels were seen as the guardians of the bodies of the saints.[69] The motif of the angels as those who guide the righteous after death is found in the New Testament in Luke xvi.22, where Lazarus is said to be carried by the angels to Abraham's bosom, and the idea was widely developed in the patristic period. Tertullian and Origen both speak of the departed soul rejoicing in seeing his angel who will lead him to paradise, and in Gregory of Nyssa's account of the death of Macrina, Macrina prays for an angel of light to guide her to the place of refreshment, the waters of comfort, and the bosom of the patriarchs.[70] The late fourth-century work, the *Apocalypse of Paul*, develops the theme of angelic guidance in more detail, incorporating such classical themes as Tartarus; Lake Acherusia, in whose milk-white waters the archangel Michael is represented as baptising repentant sinners so that they can enter heaven; and the boat-journey to paradise. Paul is represented as asking about a group of angels, about whom he is told:

> These are the angels of righteousness; they are sent to lead in the hour of their need the souls of the righteous who believed God was their helper. And I said to him: Must the righteous and the sinners meet the witnesses when they are dead? And the angel answered and said to me: There is one way by which all pass over to God, but the righteous, because they have a holy helper with them, are not troubled when they go to appear before God.[71]

The theme appears later in western burial liturgy in the antiphon 'In paradisum deducant te angeli, in tuo adventu suscipiant te martyres, et perducant te in civitatem sanctam Hierusalem'. There are many other examples in the burial liturgies, which sometimes refer to Michael in particular as the guide of departed souls and sometimes to the angels generally. Thus there is a petition in the Gelasian prayer *Opus misericordiae tuae*, Adsit ei angelus testamenti Michael;[72] in the *Liber monachorum S. Ambrosii* there is a prayer at the commendation of the soul, 'Suscipiat te sanctus Michahel archangelus, qui militiae caelestis meruit principatum: subveniant tibi sancti angeli, et perducant te in Hierusalem caelestem', which is echoed in the prayer *Deus, cui omnia vivunt* of the burial liturgy proper: 'ut suscipi iubeas animam famuli(ae) tui(ae) *ill.* per manus sanctorum angelorum tuorum deducendam in sinum amici tui Abrahae patriarchae'.[73] In the east one of the prayers in the *Apostolic Constitutions* asks that God will grant to the soul of the departed 'merciful angels',[74] and the diaconal litany of the Armenian rite prays that 'the angel of peace may hand on his spirit unto the rest of the just'.[75]

The place of rest for the righteous in these prayers is variously referred to under a number of biblical images as the heavenly Jerusalem; the waters of comfort; and as rest in the bosom of Abraham, or of the patriarchs. The expression 'in the bosom of Abraham' is derived from the reference in Luke xvi.22, where the angels are said to carry Lazarus εἰς τὸν κόλπον τοῦ Ἀβραάμ. The expression is unusual in that it does not occur in early rabbinic literature, but is clearly indicative of participation in the beatitude enjoyed by God's chosen ones, like Matthew's allusion to the heavenly banquet, when he refers to men sitting down with Abraham, Isaac, and Jacob in the kingdom of heaven.[76] Gregory of Nyssa explains the phrase as follows:

> Scripture uses 'bosom of Abraham' . . . as a symbol of the good state of the soul . . . Just as we use the word 'bosom' when referring figuratively to a part of the outline of the sea, it seems to me that Scripture uses the word 'bosom' as a symbol of the immeasurable goals towards which those who sail virtuously will come when having departed from life, they moor their souls in this good bosom as in a quiet harbour.[77]

The early church, following the example of Judaism, was very meticulous in its care for the dead. Indeed Julian the Apostate even went so far as to cite the Christian treatment of their dead as one of the reasons for their conversion of the Roman Empire.[78] The probably Jewish-Christian II Esdras promises the first place in the resurrection to those who bury dead bodies.[79] Although Augustine warns Christians not to adopt the notion found in Virgil that the unburied dead are prevented from crossing the Styx, he urges proper care for the dead, because the body is not just for ornament but belongs to the nature of man, and to care for it witnesses to a belief in the resurrection. Nevertheless, he judges that 'the care of the funeral arrangements, the establishment of the place of burial, the pomp of ceremonies—are more of a solace for the living than an aid for the dead'.[80] Lactantius also declares that Christians do not allow 'the image and workmanship of God to lie as a prey for beasts and birds', but return it 'to the earth whence it sprang'. The 'last and greatest work of piety is the burial of strangers'.[81] Many of the acts of the martyrs close with an account of the taking up of the martyr's body and its reverent burial, and though martyrs were accorded a special honour, the care over their burial would seem to reflect common Christian practice. To the details of that practice, and to the liturgical forms which accompanied burial, we must now turn.

2   *The earliest Christian burial rites*

The suspicion with which the Church was regarded by the Roman state in the first two centuries of its existence militated against the development of elaborate and magnificent burial rites, even had the Church wished to use such ceremonies. The care of the Christians for the burial of their dead was noted, but information about the details of Christian practice is not easy to obtain, for the rites of burial were not controversial matters and so did not feature in apologetic or polemical works. References to them are only incidental. The *Apostolic Tradition* of Hippolytus, at the beginning of the third century, makes no mention of rites or prayers of burial, but does include a section on 'the cemetery'. There is to be no heavy charge for the burial of the poor, but they are expected to pay the gravedigger's fee and for any tiles for the tomb.[1]

The earliest hints seem to be given us by Tertullian. In the *De Anima* he recounts a miracle which is said to have taken place when the corpse of a young girl placed its hands in an attitude of devotion 'when the priest began the appointed office'.[2] There is no indication what this office was, though it is likely that it refers to special prayers accompanying burial rather than to the eucharist. It is thought likely that the eucharist may have been celebrated at funerals in North Africa in Tertullian's day, though this can only be inferred from the references to commemorative celebrations, such as we find in the *Exhortation to chastity*. In this the phrase *pro qua oblationes annuas reddis* occurs. In the *De Monogamia*, which dates from Tertullian's Montanist period, there is a reference to the wife praying for the soul of her husband, that he may find rest, and share in the final resurrection. She is said to 'offer the Sacrifice each year on the anniversary of his falling asleep'.[3] A letter of Cyprian refers to commemorative 'oblations and sacrifices', not only for martyrs but also for confessors.[4] Tertullian also gives us a reference to the costly anointing of the Christian dead, when he writes in the *Apology* that, although Christians buy no incense, the Arabian merchants have no cause for complaint in the falling off of their trade, for 'let the Sabaeans be well assured that their more precious and costly merchandise is expended as largely in the burying of Christians as in the fumigating of gods'.[5] A later hymn of Prudentius, *Deus ignee fons animarum*, also refers to the embalming of the dead.[6]

Eusebius quotes a letter of Dionysius of Alexandria in the mid-third century in which he describes the care with which Christians buried the bodies of their fellows who had died as a result of plague.

> With willing hands they raised the bodies of the saints to their bosoms; they closed their eyes and mouths, carried them on their shoulders, and laid them out; they clung to them, embraced them, washed them, and wrapped them in grave-clothes.[7]

He contrasts this with the behaviour of the heathen, who abandoned those suffering from the plague and treated unburied corpses as dirt. Eusebius' description of the funeral of Constantine gives some indication of how a Roman imperial funeral was adapted to Christian practice. The body of the emperor, arrayed in purple, was placed in a golden coffin, which lay on a catafalque in the imperial palace, surrounded by candles in candlesticks of gold—a spectacle, Eusebius informs us with enthusiastic exaggeration, 'such as no one under the light of the sun has ever seen on earth since the world began'.[8] On the day of the funeral the body was brought in procession, preceded by detachments of soldiers and his successor Constantius, to be buried in the church of the Apostles. Constantine had previously placed there twelve sarcophagi with his own in the midst. Then, Eusebius notes, after Constantius had retired, 'the ministers of God came forward, with the multitude, and performed the rites of Divine worship with prayer'; but no further details are given.[9]

Amongst the prayers recorded by bishop Sarapion of Thmuis is one which is headed 'for one who is dead and is to be carried forth (ἐκκομιζομένον)'. This is probably to be dated between 350 and 356, and is likely to have been said in the house before the funeral. In form it is both a commendation of the soul and a prayer for the dead.

God, who hast authority of life and death (Wisd. xvi.13), God of the spirits and Master of all flesh (Numb. xvi.22), God who killest and makest alive, who bringest down to the gate of Hades and bringest up (I Sam. ii.6), who createst the spirit of man within him and takest to thyself ($\pi\alpha\rho\alpha\lambda\alpha\mu\beta\acute{\alpha}\nu\omega\nu$) the souls of the saints and givest rest, who alterest and changest and transformest thy creatures as is right and expedient, being thyself alone incorruptible, unalterable, and eternal, we beseech thee for the repose ($\kappa o\iota\mu\eta\sigma\acute{\epsilon}\omega\varsigma$) and rest of this thy servant (or this thine handmaiden): give rest to his soul, his spirit in green places ($\acute{\epsilon}\nu\ \tau\acute{o}\pi o\iota\varsigma\ \chi\lambda\acute{o}\eta\varsigma$) (cf. Ps. xxiii.2 in LXX) in chambers ($\tau\alpha\mu\iota\epsilon\acute{\iota}o\iota\varsigma$) of rest with Abraham and Isaac and Jacob and all thy saints: and raise up his body in the day which thou hast ordained, according to thy promises which cannot lie (Titus i.2), that thou mayest render to it also the heritage of which it is worthy in thy holy pastures. Remember not his transgressions and sins: and cause his departure ($\acute{\epsilon}\xi o\delta o\nu$) to be peaceable and blessed. Heal the griefs of those that pertain to him ($\tau\hat{\omega}\nu\ \delta\iota\alpha\phi\epsilon\rho\acute{o}\nu\tau\omega\nu$) with the spirit of consolation: and grant unto us all a good end through thine only-begotten Jesus Christ, through whom to thee (is) the glory and the strength in holy Spirit to the ages of ages, Amen.[10]

The tenor of the prayer, as is evident from the biblical allusions, is remarkably Jewish: indeed, until the final petition there is little to mark it as in any way a Christian prayer. The word $\acute{\epsilon}\xi o\delta o\varsigma$ is used to describe the funeral procession in the *Apostolic Constitutions*, but here it should most probably be translated as 'departure'. There is unlikely to be any explicit paschal reference.[11]

We have another description of burial in an apocryphal infancy narrative written in Garshuni between 385 and 395, which describes the burial of Elisabeth. According to this account, while Jesus was with his parents in Egypt, John the Baptist and his mother Elisabeth wandered through the desert, where Elisabeth died. John did not know how to shroud and bury her, so Jesus, Mary, and Salome miraculously flew on a cloud to 'Ain Karim to help.

Then the Saviour said to his virgin mother: 'Arise, you and Salome, and wash the body.' And they washed the body of the blessed Elisabeth . . . Then Michael and Gabriel came down from heaven and dug a grave; and the Saviour said to them: 'Go and bring the soul of Zacharias, and the soul of the priest Simeon, in order that they may sing while you bury the body.' And Michael brought immediately the souls of Zacharias and Simeon, who shrouded the body of Elisabeth and sang for a long time over it . . .[12]

It is the reference to singing which is of particular interest, as this is later referred to as characteristic of Christian funerals. In *Apostolic Constitutions* vi.30, after warnings about not following Jewish ideas about uncleanness resulting from touching a dead body, Christians are exhorted to read the scriptures and sing 'for the martyrs which are fallen asleep, and for all the saints from the beginning of the world, and for your brethren that are asleep in the Lord'. 'And in the funerals of the departed, accompany them with singing, if they were faithful in Christ.' Jerome, in his description of the funeral of the lady Paula, writes that 'no weeping or lamentation followed her death, such as are the custom of the world; but all present united in chanting the psalms in their several tongues'.[13] And at the funeral of Fabiola 'psalms were chanted and the gilded ceilings of the temples were shaken with uplifted shouts of Alleluia'.[14] Anthony is said to chant 'hymns and psalms in the Christian manner' as he buries the body of Paul the hermit.[15] Chanting of psalms is also noted by Socrates in his account of the translation of the body of Babylas from Daphne to Antioch, only in this case 'the psalms were such as cast reproach on the gods of the heathen and those who put confidence in them and their images'.[16]

The funeral psalms are identified by Chrysostom as xxii, xxiii and cxvi.[17] At the funeral of the Novatian bishop of Constantinople in 438 Christians of all parties united for the funeral and 'all attended his body to the tomb chanting psalms'.[18] This singing of psalms and hymns is seen as a contrast to the wailing and lamentation of pagan rites. Chrysostom forbids the hiring of professional mourning women, and condemns Christian women for uttering wild cries and tearing their clothes at funerals. Grief may indeed be shown, but Christian grief should not be such as to show lack of faith in the resurrection, but merely because the separation is hard to bear. 'Weep, then, at the death of a dear one as if you were bidding farewell to one setting out on a journey.' 'Honour for the dead,' he continues, 'does not consist in lamentations and moanings, but in singing hymns and psalms and living a noble life', for the departed goes on his way in the company of the angels, even if no one is present at his funeral. Likewise all exaggerated funeral pomp, rich grave-clothes, and sumptuous trappings should be eschewed. A simple shroud for the body and the giving of alms as a memorial were all that was needful.[19]

There are likewise efforts to replace the *vestes sordidae* of paganism by white garments expressive of Christian hope. The black, or sometimes red, which was characteristic of pagan mourning dress, and which eventually triumphed even in the Church as the colour of the liturgy of the dead, was not originally indicative of an absolutely black material, but referred rather to the natural colour of the wool from which the garments were made after it had been soiled through being rolled in the dirt and sprinkled with dust and ashes, as was customary in pagan mourning.[20] Such practices were regarded as unsuitable for Christians to follow. Cyprian, in *De Mortalitate*, forbids the putting on of dark garments by those who mourn the dead who have already put on white garments in heaven.[21] Basil urges Christians to cease lamentation and wailing, the rending of garments and the spreading of ashes.[22] Ephraem Syrus and Chrysostom do the same. 'Let not her (the Church's) deceased be buried in the cutting off of hope heathenishly, with vestments and wailing and lamentation; for the living is clothed in raiment, but the deceased, his all is a coffin.'[23] 'Finally, why do we dye our garments black if not to show that we are truly unbelievers and wretched, not only by our wailing but even by our clothing?'[24]

Although the Church eventually lost this battle, it would appear that in the early centuries Christian funerals were frequently triumphant and dignified and indicative of hope. Gregory of Nyssa, in his funeral oration on Meletius, talks of 'the streams of fire from the succession of lamps', which 'flowed along in an unbroken track of light, and extended so far that the eye could not reach them', and he speaks of a similar procession at the funeral of his sister Macrina.[25] Although it became traditional for the bier of the deceased to be carried in the funeral procession by those of the same order as that to which the deceased had belonged, this rule was not one which was invariably followed. Macrina is said to have had bishops amongst her bearers at her funeral, and Jerome records the same of Paula, though with obvious exaggeration.

> The bishops lifted up the dead woman with their own hands, placed her upon a bier, and carrying her on their shoulders to the church in the cave of the Saviour, laid her down in the centre of it. Other bishops meantime carried torches and tapers in the procession, and yet others led the singing of choirs. The whole population of the cities of Palestine came to the funeral.[26]

Writing of the funeral of Blaesilla, Jerome notes that her bier was covered with cloth of gold, and that her funeral procession was headed by people of rank.[27] But cloth of gold was not usual at funerals, and sumptuousness in funeral arrangements was frequently condemned. Augustine, for instance, warns against imitating the lavish funeral rites of the rich, who expire on ivory beds and are born to their graves amidst the mourning of their entire household establishment.[28]

Augustine's account of his mother's funeral is indicative of the simplicity and quiet joy which is apparent in nearly all the accounts of early Christian funerals which have come down to us. The first action after Monnica's death was for Augustine to close her eyes, and although, he writes, he wished to give expression to his grief, he 'repressed it with a man's voice, the voice of my heart was silent', for it was not fitting that her funeral should be marked by the weeping and lamentation of those who considered death to be but misery and destruction. Evodius then began the recitation of Psalm ci, *Misericordiam et iudicium*, 'to which all in the house made answer'. Monnica's body was then prepared for burial.

> And behold, the corpse was carried to the burial; we went and returned without tears. For neither in those prayers which we poured forth unto thee, when the sacrifice of our ransom was offered for her, when now the corpse was by the grave's side, as the manner there is, previous to its being laid therein, did I weep even during those prayers.[29]

Augustine further records Monnica's own wishes as to the manner of her burial.

> For she, when the day of her death drew near, did not crave that her body might be sumptuously adorned, or embalmed with spices, nor desired she any choice monument, or to be buried in her own land. These things she did not recommend to us, but desired only to be remembered at thy altar whereat she used to assist without intermission of one day.[30]

Occasional references occur later to complaints about exorbitant funeral charges. A good example is to be found in a letter of Gregory the Great to Januarius, bishop of Caralis.

> The most distinguished lady Nereida complained to us that your Fraternity does not blush to exact from her a hundred *solidi* for the burial of her daughter, and would bring upon her the additional vexation of expense over and above her groans of sorrow. Now, if the truth is so, it being a very serious thing and far from a priest's office to require a price for earth that is granted to rottenness, and to wish to make profit out of another's grief, let your Fraternity refrain from this

demand and be no more troublesome to her . . . Now as to this abuse, we ourselves, after we had by God's permission acceded to the dignity of the episcopate, forbade it entirely in our church, and by no means permitted the evil custom to be taken up anew . . . But if at any time you allow any one to be buried in your church, and the parents, relations, or heirs of such persons should of their own accord wish to offer something for lights, we do not forbid it to be accepted.[31]

Incense, as it would appear from Tertullian's comments, does not seem to have been used at Christian funerals in the first two centuries, but by the fifth century the use of it was gradually established, the earliest clear instance of its use being at the funeral of St Honoratus in Gaul in 430.[32] In the funeral procession, according to Chrysostom, palm and olive branches were carried, and not the funerary cypresses of pagan practice. Evergreen laurel and ivy were sometimes placed in the coffin as emblems of immortality.[33]

The Apostolic Constitutions

The *Apostolic Constitutions* provide us with considerable information about Christian burial. The collection, as we have it, is generally considered to have originated in Syria about the year 380, but the eight books of which it is composed consist of earlier material, which has been worked over and added to by a redactor who is thought to have had Arian tendencies. In Book VI there is a brief reference to burial practice which is substantially the same as that which occurs in the latter part of the *Didascalia Apostolorum*, a work which is usually dated in the first half of the third century. The author of the *Didascalia* is particularly concerned to prevent Christians from following the ritual prescriptions of Judaism, and discusses burial practice in this context, insisting that Christians are not to regard contact with a dead body as something which in any way defiles them. The section in which this is discussed indicates that by the time the *Didascalia* was written it was customary to celebrate the eucharist at funerals, as well as on the anniversary of death.

Do you according to the Gospel, and according to the power of the Holy Spirit, come together even in the cemeteries, and read the holy Scriptures, and without demur perform your ministry and your supplication to God; and offer an acceptable eucharist, the likeness of the royal body of Christ, both in your congregations and in your cemeteries, and on the departures of them that sleep—pure bread that is made with fire and sanctified with invocations—and without doubting pray and offer for them that are fallen asleep?[34]

This statement is repeated in the sixth book of the *Apostolic Constitutions*, with the addition of references to singing, which we have already noted. Immediately afterwards the author of the *Constitutions* quotes four verses of scripture, which may possibly have been part of a burial office. These are Psalm cxvi.13, 'Precious in the sight of the Lord is the death of his saints'; Psalm cxvi.7, 'O my soul, return unto thy rest, for the Lord hath done thee good'; Proverbs x.7, 'The memory of the righteous is a blessing'; and Wisdom iii.1, 'The souls of the righteous are in the hands of God'.[35] Psalm cxvi is a common feature of later burial offices. It occurs, amongst other places, in the Armenian rite, both at the arrival at the place of burial and when the body is placed in the grave, with verse 7 being said as the *ktorzd* on the first occasion; at the beginning of the Coptic rite, and in part (vv.5, 6 and 7) as the prayer of the Gospel in the variant services for women and male children; in the group of prayers to be said after the soul has left the body in one of the earliest Western liturgies of burial (Cologne MS 123); and as one of the psalms in the funeral procession from the place of death to the church in the eighth- or ninth-century manuscript, Rheinau 30. It is also found as one of the psalms to be said during the commendation of the soul and preparation of the body in the York and Sarum rites, and as the first of the group of psalms to be said 'in the churche either before or after the buriall of the corps' in the Prayer Book of 1549.[36]

There are further references to Christian care of the departed in Book VIII of the *Apostolic Constitutions*. Section xli contains prayers for use at the burial of the dead, though, as H.-R. Philippeau has pointed out, there is no evidence that the liturgy as it is given there was ever used in any ancient oriental church.[37] Whether this be the case or not, the themes of the prayers are familiar ones, and reflect the same outlook as the prayer given in Serapion's collection. In both instances God is addressed as the One who is the Lord and creator of life, who is alone immortal, and who calls men to Him at death. Both prayers ask that God will grant the departed forgiveness, fellowship with the patriarchs and all the saints, and enjoyment of the peace and joy of paradise.

The burial liturgy of the *Apostolic Constitutions* instructs the deacon after the bidding prayer to pray as follows:

> Let us pray for our brethren that are at rest in Christ, that God, the lover of mankind, who has received his soul, may forgive him every sin, voluntary and involuntary, and may be merciful and gracious to him, and give him his lot in the land of the pious that are sent into the bosom of Abraham, and Isaac, and Jacob, with all those that have pleased him and done his will from the beginning of the world, whence all sorrow, grief, and lamentation are banished.
>
> Let us arise, let us dedicate ourselves and one another to the eternal God, through that Word which was in the beginning.

Then the bishop offers a similar prayer.

> O thou who art by nature immortal, and hast no end of thy being, from whom every creature, whether immortal or mortal, is derived; who didst make man a rational creature, the citizen of this world, in his constitution mortal, and didst add the promise of a resurrection; who didst not suffer Enoch and Elias to taste of death; 'the God of Abraham, the God of Isaac, and the God of Jacob, who art the God of them, not as of dead, but as of living persons: for the souls of all men live with thee, and the spirits of the righteous are in thy hand, which no torment can touch'; for they are all sanctified under thy hand: do thou now also look upon this thy servant, whom thou hast selected and received into another state, and forgive him if voluntarily or involuntarily he has sinned, and afford him merciful angels, and place him in the bosom of the patriarchs, and prophets, and apostles, and of all those that have pleased thee from the beginning of the world, where there is no grief, sorrow, nor lamentation; but the peaceable region of the godly, and the undisturbed land of the upright, and of those that therein see the glory of thy Christ; by whom glory, honour and worship, thanksgiving and adoration be to thee, in the Holy Spirit, for ever. Amen.

The deacon then says, 'Bow down and receive the blessing', and the bishop then 'gives thanks' for them.

> O Lord, save thy people, and bless thine inheritance, which thou hast purchased with the precious blood of thy Christ. Feed them under thy right hand, and cover them under thy wings, and grant that they may 'fight the good fight, and finish their course, and keep the faith' immutably, unblamably, and unreprovably, through our Lord Jesus Christ, thy beloved Son, with whom glory, honour, and worship be to thee and to the Holy Spirit for ever. Amen.[38]

The following two sections of Book VIII provide for the observance of the anniversary days of the departed, and for the giving of alms to the poor from the dead man's estate as a memorial of him, and warn against participating in the drunken orgies which frequently accompanied pagan memorial feasts.[39]

The Ecclesiastical Hierarchy

It is again a probably Syrian source which gives us, a century or more later than the compilation of the *Apostolic Constitutions*, further details of the development of the liturgy of burial in Eastern Christendom. The work in question is the *Ecclesiastical Hierarchy* (Περὶ τῆς ἐκκλησιαστικῆς ἱεραρχίας), one of the mystical works of pseudo-Dionysius the Areopagite. Although in the Middle Ages it was thought to date, with the rest of the Dionysian corpus, from the first century, it is now considered to have been written *c.* 500 somewhere in the region of Syria. The *Ecclesiastical Hierarchy* is a parallel work to the author's *Celestial Hierarchy*, and treats of the sacraments, of the clergy, and of the laity, as images of the hierarchy of being indwelt by the Divine Light. It is in the final section of the *Ecclesiastical Hierarchy* that the burial rites are described under the title of the 'Mystery over those who have fallen asleep in holiness'.[40] The section begins with a long description of the joy with which the saints embrace their death, which ends as follows:

> The just man is full of holy gladness when he comes to the end of his warfare, and it is with great joy that he advances towards his new life. His acquaintance, his neighbours in God, whose lives resemble his own, congratulate him on having attained the victory and goal of his desires. They sing hymns of thanksgiving in honour of him who is the author of this victory, asking him to grant them also the grace of such a repose. Then they take the body of the dead and carry it to the bishop as if for the award of the crown of victory. The latter receives it with joy and, in accordance with the rules, performs the second rites instituted for those who have died a holy death.[41]

Then the author gives a description of the rite itself. The body of the departed is placed at the foot of the altar, if the dead man be a priest; if he is a monk or a layman his body remains outside the sanctuary. The bishop then begins the prayer of thanksgiving, which is followed by reading of 'the faithful promises contained in the divine Scripture on the subject of our resurrection' done by the deacon. Psalms relating to the same theme are then sung, and after this the catechumens are dismissed. In the 'Contemplation' which follows the description of the rite, the author notes that this dismissal of the catechumens is a variation on the usual practice, by which penitents were also excluded.

> Notice this, however. In this ceremony, instead of sending out, as usually happens, all those who belong to the order of those undergoing purification, only the catechumens are excluded from the congregation. These latter, being not yet initiated into any of the sacraments, could not assist without irreverence, however little, at any of the ceremonies of the sacred liturgy; for God is not yet born in them, he who is the source and distributor of light, and so they have not yet received in any degree the power of contemplating the mysteries. On the other hand the rest of those undergoing purification have already been initiated and received the sacred gifts . . . If they were to participate unworthily in these sacred ceremonies (i.e. the eucharist) they would suffer for their audacity and would only increase their contempt of divine realities and due consideration for themselves. None the less, it is lawful to admit them to the funeral rites, for this spectacle teaches them clearly the uncertainty of the hour of death, the rewards promised to the good by the infallible Scriptures, and the punishment without end with which they threaten the wicked.[42]

After the dismissal of the catechumens the description of the rite continues:

> The principal deacon . . . reads the names of those who have already died a holy death, estimating him who has just finished his earthly life as worthy to be commemorated with them and like them. Finally, he exhorts all those present to pray for an ultimate happiness in Christ. The divine bishop then recites a prayer over the body. When this is finished, he kisses the dead, followed in this immediately by all present. When all have given the kiss of peace, the bishop anoints the body with holy oil and prays for all the dead. He then places the body in holy ground by the side of other saints of equal dignity.[43]

The 'Contemplation' informs us that the bishop's prayer asks God 'to pardon the dead all the faults due to human weakness and to establish him in the light and land of the living, in the bosom of Abraham, Isaac, and Jacob, where sorrow, sadness and weeping are known no more'. The customary reference to the bosom of the patriarchs is explained by the author as meaning 'the divine repose and perfect happiness encompassing all those who live in conformity with God in perfect happiness without end'.[44] The anointing of the body is again referred to in the 'Contemplation'.

> After the kiss of peace the bishop anoints the body of the dead with holy oil. You will remember that in the ceremony of birth from God it

is, before baptism, by anointing with holy oil that the initiate is permitted for the first time to participate in the sacred symbols, immediately after he has been stripped of his former dress. Now, on the contrary, it is at the end of all that holy oil is poured out over the dead. Then the sacred anointing summoned the initiate to a holy warfare; now the pouring of the oil signifies that in this combat he has fought to victory.[45]

As Rutledge notes in his commentary on the *Ecclesiastical Hierarchy*, this anointing has nothing to do with the sacrament of unction, but is part of the sacramental action of preparing the body for burial. Dionysius clearly connects it with the anointing of baptism, and this parallel between baptism and burial is one which is also worked out in other early burial rites by their use of exodus psalmody with its paschal and baptismal significance.

The anointing of the dead is also found in the Western Church. The Penitential of archbishop Theodore of Canterbury, himself a Greek from Tarsus, which dates from the seventh century, mentions that it is the custom of the Roman Church to anoint the bodies of monks and religious men, and the same use is also referred to in the paraphrase of the Penitential of Halitgar, bishop of Cambrai in the ninth century, which was added to the eighth-century Penitential of Egbert of York.[46] The Penitential of Theodore interestingly has a reference to Dionysius in the same section.[47] This anointing of the dead is still a characteristic of the modern Greek liturgy of burial, the oil being poured on the body after it has been laid in the grave. In the case of priests the body is anointed with holy oil on the forehead, mouth, breast, hands, and feet immediately after death, whereas the bodies of laymen are merely washed with water. If the sacrament of unction has been given before death, the oil used is that which remains; if not, it is taken from one of the lamps in the church.[48]

3 *Traditional Eastern rites*

The pattern of burial liturgy indicated by the *Ecclesiastical Hierarchy* was developed and elaborated in the Eastern Church. In particular, different services were devised for the burial of clergy and laity, and in some traditions these forms themselves were varied in a more minute way. Thus the Coptic rite provides special services (the main variants being in lections and psalmody) for male children; adult women; female children; women dying in childbirth; patriarchs, metropolitans, and bishops; hegumens and priests; deacons, monks, and nuns; as well as orders of service for both men and women who die during Holy Week, during which time the use of incense and prayers for the dead are prohibited.[1] Through the multiplication of psalmody and hymns many of these eastern rites also became very lengthy, so that their basic structure is not always immediately discernible. It must be born in mind, however, that many of the additions appear to have arisen from the practical need to provide sufficient texts to cover the ceremonies of washing and preparing the body for burial, and the funeral processions from the house to the church and from the church to the place of burial.

The eastern rites, as they have evolved, are all marked by a basically similar pattern, corresponding to the stages of taking the body from the place of death to the church and then to the place of burial, where finally it is laid in the tomb and the grave is filled in or the tomb sealed. Thus we find (1) an *introductory section* of prayers and responses, and often of psalmody, which intended to be said in the house. Then follows (2) the *funeral procession to the church*, during which psalms—or liturgical chants based on psalms—are recited. At the church, or sometimes at the tomb, if the procession goes straight there, there is (3) a *service of prayers, hymns, and psalmody*, with usually two passages of Scripture read as epistle and gospel. There may then be a ritual farewell, such as the last kiss in the Greek rite, or this may take place only when the procession reaches the grave, as in the East Syrian

('Nestorian') *Kahneita*. Further psalmody, anthems or responses are provided to cover (4) the *procession from the church to the place of burial*. The *burial* itself (5) is usually a simple act of committal, marked by short prayers of commendation and the sprinkling of earth on the body. This is the basic pattern, though within this there are many variations of details between the different rites.

The Byzantine Order

The Byzantine rite is contained in the *Euchologion*. It begins with a service at the house where the death has occurred.[2] The priest, vested in stole, censes the body and begins the service with the priestly blessing. Then follow, in a manner similar to the introductory section of Greek Matins, the *Trisagion*, *Gloria*, *Triadikon*,[3] three-fold *Kyrie*, *Gloria* and Lord's Prayer, concluded with the doxology said by the priest. A *Doxastikon*[4] and *Theotokion*[5] are then said, the words of the *troparia* consisting of prayers that the soul of the departed may be granted rest with the righteous (μετὰ πνευμάτων δικαίων) and that the Lord who descended into hell will give rest to the one who has died (Σύ ἐι ὁ Θεὸς ὁ καταβὰς ἐισᾷδην). After the *Troparia* the deacon, if present, says a short litany, whilst the priest recites the prayer for the departed, Ὁ Θεὸς τῶν πνευμάτων καὶ πάσης σάρκος, which occurs here for the first of many times in the burial office. The priest's prayer concludes with a doxology said out loud. 'For thou art the Resurrection and the Life', after which the deacon proclaims 'Wisdom', the choir sing the *Theotokion*, τὴν τιμιωτέραν τῶν Χερουβὶμ. The first part of the service ends at this point.

When all is ready for the procession to the church, there is a repetition of the priestly blessing and *Trisagion* as at the beginning of the service. The funeral procession then commences with Psalm xci being said, followed by Psalm cxix. This comprises one of the 'stichologies' into which the Psalter is divided in the Greek Office, and is said, as in the office, in three sections (vv. 1–72; 73–132; 133–176). Each is followed by a prayer, in this case the diaconal litany for the departed, and the prayer Ὁ Θεὸς τῶν πνευμάτων καὶ πάσῆς σάρκος. 'Alleluia' is said as a response after each verse of the first and third sections, and 'Have mercy upon thy servant' as the response after the verses of the second section. It is now quite usual, however, for only the first and last verses of each section of the psalm, with their appropriate responses to be said.

The third part of the service, which takes place in the church, is made up of five sections, the Funeral Blessing, the Funeral Canon, the Anthem, the Beatitudes, the reading of Scripture, and the final leave-taking. The Funeral Blessing consists of five *troparia*, with the refrain 'Blessed art thou, O Lord; teach me thy statutes', followed by a *Doxastikon*, then the diaconal litany for the departed, and then a second *Doxastikon*, beginning Ἀνάπαυσον Σωτὴρ ἡμῶν μετὰ δικαίων, 'Give rest, O our Saviour, with the righteous'. Psalm li is then recited, immediately before the Canon as in the order for Matins. The Funeral Canon, whose authorship is ascribed to the ninth-century author Theophanes Graptos, is constructed on the same principle as all Greek Canons, namely a series of Odes, consisting of *troparia* based on biblical canticles, each Ode beginning with the *Hirmos*, a *troparion* from which those which follow derive both their rhyme and their chant. There are eight odes in all, the second ode out of the full series of nine being omitted except in the Canons for the Great Lent. There are breaks after the third and sixth odes, the first break being marked by the litany for the departed and the *Kathisma*,[6] and the second by the *Kontakion* for the departed and the *Ikos*.[7] The litany for the departed and the prayer Ὁ Θεὸς τῶν πνευμάτων καὶ πάσης σάρκος occur again at the end of the Canon. The eight odes of the Canon are largely concerned with God's saving acts, and the martyrs as those who are the exemplars of Christian death. Their particular themes are as follows:

1. *Hirmos:* Israel's crossing of the Red Sea.
   Troparia: the prayers of the martyrs; man's creation and fall; petitions for the departed.
2. *Hirmos:* the holiness and salvation of God.
   Troparia: the martyrs; the compassion of God; petition for the departed; a concluding *Theotokion*.
3. *Hirmos:* the confidence of the believer in Christ.
   Troparia: the martyrs; petitions that the departed may be received into the light and glory of Christ.
4. *Hirmos:* the light of Christ victorious over sin.
   Troparia: the sacrifice of the martyrs; prayer for the departed, that he may be brought to the heavenly mansions and the kingdom of God.
5. *Hirmos:* God, the merciful Deliverer from the storms of the sea of life.
   Troparia: the martyrs' imitation of the Passion of Christ; prayer for

deliverance at the coming of Christ, and for the attainment of paradise.

6. *Hirmos:* the deliverance from the burning, fiery furnace.
   Troparia: the sacrifice of the martyrs; prayer for the departed to Christ the life-giver.
7. *Hirmos:* the deliverance from the burning, fiery furnace.
   Troparia: the victory of the martyrs; prayer for those whose lives have shown the victory of faith.
8. *Hirmos:* Christ the revealer of the ineffable Godhead.
   Troparia: the hope of the martyrs; prayer for the enlightenment and rest of the departed.

The Funeral Canon is followed by the Anthem, the hymn of John Damascene, Ποία τοῦ βίου τρυφὴ. This is in eight stanzas, the first of which is known in the English translation of Athelstan Riley as the hymn 'What sweet of life endureth unmixed with bitter pain.' Each of the stanzas is appropriated to a different musical tone. After the Anthem the Beatitudes are sung interspersed with *troparia* asking for deliverance from the destruction and agony of death, and concluding with a Theotokion. Then follows the reading of Scripture. The *Prokimenon* (Gradual) is read, Μακαρία ἡ ὁδὸς ᾗ πορεύῃ σήμερον, 'Blessed is the way in which you shall walk today', and the Epistle (I Thessalonians iv.13–18) and Gospel (John v.24–30), with the customary introductions and conclusions as in the Liturgy. The deacon again recites the litany for the departed, and the prayer, Ὁ Θεὸς τῶν πνευμάτων καὶ πάσης σάρκος, is said out loud. This brings us to the last section of the service in church, the final leave-taking of the dead, symbolized in the giving of the last kiss. The congregation approach the open coffin and bestow the kiss on the body of the departed, whilst the hymn Δεῦτε τελεύταιον ἀσπασμὸν δῶμεν, ἀδελφοὶ, 'Come, brethren, let us give the last kiss to the dead', is sung, followed by a *Theotokion* asking the prayers of the Virgin for the one who has departed, and a hymn written as though in the person of the departed asking for those present to pray for him. After a second *Theotokion*, the *Trisagion*, *Gloria*, *Triadikon*, *Kyries* and Lord's Prayer are said, concluding with the litany for the departed and the prayer Ὁ Θεὸς τῶν πνευμάτων καὶ πάσης σάρκος. A blessing is then given, Ὁ ἀναστὰς ἐκ νεκρῶν, Χρίστος, modelled on the final blessing of the *Liturgy of St John Chrysostom*, but with special petitions at the end that the soul of the departed may dwell in the mansions of the righteous; may be given rest in the bosom of Abraham; and may be numbered amongst the righteous. A final sentence is then said, which is repeated three times, Ἀ'ωνία σοῦ ἡ μνήμη ἀξιομακάριστε καὶ ἀείμνηστε ἀδελφὲ ἡμῶν. 'May your memory be eternal, O brother of ours, you who are worthy to be blessed and had in everlasting remembrance'.

This concludes the service in church. A second procession is then formed, which escorts the body to the place of burial, whilst the *Trisagion*, *Gloria*, *Triadikon*, *Kyries* and Lord's Prayer are said. On arrival at the place of burial the body is placed in the grave, and the priest sprinkles it with earth in the form of a cross, saying as he does so, 'The earth is the Lord's and the fulness thereof; the whole world, and they who dwell in it.' The grave is then filled up with the earth whilst a *Doxastikon* is sung, praying for rest for the departed. This concludes the rite of burial, and also the funeral liturgy.

The Greek burial rite for priests contains some significant differences from that for the laity. At death the body is prepared for burial by three priests, who rub it all over with oil, and then clothe it in the sacerdotal vestments. The face is covered with a chalice-veil and the book of the Gospels is laid on the breast. The rite then proceeds almost exactly as for lay burial until the end of the Funeral Blessing. There then follows a group of three short *troparia* known as an *Anabathmos*,[8] which lead in to a series of four pairs of lessons, each consisting of an epistle and a gospel, preceded by a *Prokimenon* (Gradual), and followed by *troparia* and psalmody. The lessons and psalmody are as follows: (i) I Thessalonians iv.13–18; John v.24–30; Psalm xxiii with intercalated Alleluias; (ii) Romans v.12–22; John v.17–25; Psalm xxiv with Alleluias; (iii) I Corinthians xv.1–12; John vi.35–39; Psalm lxxxiv with Alleluias; (iv) I Corinthians xv.20–29; John vi.48–54. The prayers which follow the first three groups of readings all contain petitions for the repose of the soul of the departed in the bosom of the patriarchs. The fourth group of readings is followed immediately by the Beatitudes, though the intercalated verses differ from those in the rite of lay burial. Then, as in the office for laymen, there follows the *Prokimenon*, Epistle (Romans xiv.6–9) and Gospel (John vi.48–54), and, after this, Psalm li. This leads into the Funeral Canon, which deals with many of the same themes as that in the rite of lay burial, but uses for the most part different *Hirmoi* and *Troparia*. The *Kontakion* for the departed is identical, but the succeeding *Ikos* is both different and much lengthier. At the end of the Canon a short sequence of responses known as the *Exaposteilarion*[9] is prescribed, which is followed by a series of *Stichera* (Verses) beginning Θεοποιηθεὶς ἐν τῇ μεταστάσει, τῷ ζωοποίῳ σοῦ νῦν μυστηρίῳ, πρὸς σὲ μεταβέβηκεν. The *Gloria in excelsis* is then recited, and after that the hymn of St John Damascene Ποῖα τοῦ βιόυ τρυφὴ, in a much expanded version. The *Troparion*, Ἀνάπαυσον Σῶτηρ ἡμῶν, μετὰ Δικαίων, which in the lay rite occurs as the second *Doxastikon* after the Funeral Blessings, is then sung, and the Last Kiss is given, as in the order for laymen. From this point to the end of the funeral liturgy the two rites are the same, with the exception that part of the Great Canon of St Andrew of Crete is prescribed for the procession from the church to the place of burial in the case of priests.

The funeral liturgy for the clergy is closer to the pattern of the morning office than the rite of lay burial. There are some general structural parallels between the service at the house in both rites and the beginning of Matins (with the exception of the psalmody) which commences with *Trisagion*, Lord's prayer, *troparia*, litany-prayer, priestly blessing, the great collect and the verses and *troparia* of the day. The Psalm of the funeral procession corresponds to the Stichology of the Psalter, being divided in a similar way. The burial rite for priests then has an *Anabathmos*, which follows the Stichology of the Psalter at Matins, and, after the addition of the Beatitudes, there is an epistle and gospel corresponding to the Matins Gospel of Sundays and Feast Days. Psalm li follows on in both offices, and then the Canon, with the *Exaposteilarion* at the end. There is again a parallel in the στίχηρα of the Funeral Office, which are found where the στίχηρα of the feast would be in the Matins order, and in both instances they are succeeded by the *Gloria in excelsis*.

The date of the rite as we have it is difficult to determine exactly without further detailed research. The procession with psalmody, and some kind of rite at the house during the preparation of the body for burial would seem to be early features, but much of the office appointed to be said in the church cannot go back further than the seventh or eighth century. The 'prayer of thanksgiving' referred to by the pseudo-Dionysius may indicate an early form of the Funeral Blessing, and his reference to the reading of 'the faithful promises contained in the divine Scripture on the subject of our resurrection' indicates that the Scriptural lessons are an early feature. The Funeral Canon cannot be earlier than the seventh century, in which the Canon first became part of the Daily Office, but if the ascription to Theophanes be accurate it is even later, Theophanes' dates being 759–*c*.842. The hymn of John Damascene, Ποία τοῦ βίου τρυφὴ, was most probably written at the beginning of the eighth century, but is not likely to have become established as a regular feature of the burial liturgy until some time later than this. The practice of giving the Last Kiss as a farewell to the departed is, as we have seen, one of considerable antiquity with its roots in pagan practice, but the hymns and prayers prescribed to accompany it are later.

It is the prayer, ὁ Θεος τῶν πνευμάτων καὶ πάσης σάρκος which recurs so many times in the Greek funeral liturgy, which is to be reckoned amongst the earliest texts contained in the rite. As will be seen from the table on page 53f., this prayer belongs to a common tradition of burial prayers in the Eastern liturgies. All these prayers, with the exception of that in the *Apostolic Constitutions*, which draws on other themes and only very partially reflects the common tradition, contain similar petitions and incorporate the same scriptural quotation in their phraseology, the most common texts being Numbers xvi.22; Psalm xxiii.2; I Samuel ii.6; Wisdom iii.1; xvi.13; Matthew xxii.32; I Timothy vi.16; and Revelation xxi.4. The occurrence of this pattern of funeral prayer in the sacramentary of Sarapion takes it back to the fourth century, and there is another early example of it in the post-communion intercessions in the *Liturgy of St James*. If this is the prayer referred to by Cyril of Jerusalem as being offered for the departed at this point in his description of the Jerusalem liturgy of his day, this would also link it with the fourth-century Jerusalem church.[10] Of the prayers whose text is given, it is the Armenian which resembles that in the Greek rite of lay burial most closely, and it is probably directly derived from it. The Coptic, as might perhaps be expected, follows the themes of the various petitions in the prayer of Sarapion more closely than the others, though with a number of additions and, curiously, without any reference to Numbers xvi.22, the text which is most generally characteristic of these Eastern prayers.

The Armenian Order

The Armenian rite, which bears the title of the 'Canon for the burial of all and sundry that have died',[11] falls into six sections:

37

(1) a service of psalmody, readings, and prayers held either in church or at the house of the deceased; (2) the funeral procession to the place of burial; (3) a short office at the grave-side; (4) the committal; (5) the final sealing of the grave; and (6) the return to the house of the deceased, where prayers are offered. The first office begins with a *Gobola* of three psalms (cxxviii, xxx or lxxi, cxli or cxlii), followed by the *Kyrie* repeated forty times. The priest then reads a long prayer, which recalls God's mercy in man's creation and redemption, and in the promise of the resurrection, and asks God to show his continuing mercy by receiving the soul of the departed:

> And now O Lord, kind and merciful, do thou receive the soul of this man, who has fulfilled the time of his sojourning as a stranger upon earth, and has received release from his toil.
>
> Rank him with thy saints in thy kingdom, from which is absent all pain and sorrow and lamentations; so that he may ever rejoice and exult, being made resplendent by the vision of thy divine glory, where all the chosen ones do rejoice. With them give rank and place, O Lord, to the soul of our departed one, so that we, in company with him, may glorify Father and Son and holy Spirit, now and ever, and to eternity of eternities, Amen.

A further prayer is said with the same intent, after which Psalm xxix is repeated 'in tones of lamentation', with the verse 'Behold with a measure thou hast set out my days' as *ktorzd* (antiphon). The lesson (II Corinthians i.3–11) is then read, followed by Psalm cxlii, and the Gospel (John v.19–30), which is the same as that in the Greek rite with the addition of five verses at the beginning. The burial prayer, 'God of spirits', is then said, followed by a second prayer for the peace and rest of the departed. On the assumption that what has so far been done is at the house of the departed, there next occurs the rubric that 'if the deceased be one of the clerks, or of the penitents, or a leading master of a house, they carry him to the door of the church', where, either on their way there or on arrival, is said Psalm lxxxiv with the *ktorzd* 'Blessed are they that dwell in the house of the Lord'. A second lesson (I Thessalonians iv.13–18, as in the Greek rite) and a second Gospel (a conflation of Luke x and Matthew xi) are then read, followed by a litany for the departed and two further prayers very similar in character to the traditional eastern burial prayer. This concludes the first part of the rite.

The second section consists of the funeral procession to the place of burial, during which, as in the funeral procession from the house to the church in the Greek rite, Psalm cxix is recited. Two hymns are also prescribed for the procession. The third division of the service, the office at the tomb, has much the same form as the first, namely a psalm (cxvi), a lesson (I Corinthians xv.12–25), three-fold Alleluia, the Gospel (John xii.24–26), and the prayer 'God of spirits'. This is followed by a prayer which reflects on the events of the Last Day, and prays for God's mercy on the departed. The body is then placed in the tomb, Psalm cxvi is again repeated, followed by *Gloria in excelsis* and a litany for the departed and for those who mourn, ending with the response 'Our souls we commit: have mercy upon us' and the Kyrie repeated a hundred times. After this the priest says the 'Prayer of the Sealing of the Sepulchre', which begins with a reference to man's existence in the paradise of Eden at creation and goes on to ask that God will receive the soul of the departed:

> And now, Lord, our beneficent God, receive thy servant here, who hath fulfilled the period of his sojourn upon earth, and according to thy commandment hath drawn nigh to enter into the womb of the earth from which he is to be born again. And now Lord our God, do thou stretch forth thy protecting right hand, and seal the place of his rest. And do thou bring near his spirit, which thou hast consigned and committed into the hand of thy angel, unto the throne of thy holy glory, in company with the other shining souls to rejoice and exult and circle in the dance around thy royal throne, until the day of thy second coming from heaven in the glory of the Father and of all the holy angels; when thou shalt come again to renew and set up afresh thy image . . .

A second prayer follows, and then a hymn, which concludes the service at the tomb. The congregation then returns to the house of the deceased where Psalm xliv is said and a prayer for the consolation of all who mourn.

As with all the Eastern rites there is a separate liturgy for the burial of priests.[12] This is extremely lengthy and consists of a number of 'canons', short offices made up of a psalm, several (usually fairly short) lessons concluding with a passage from a Gospel, and then a lengthy prayer for the departed. The first of these canons is appointed to be said when the site of the grave is marked out by the sign of the cross being traced in the earth. The second provides an office for the washing of the body, with appropriate lessons from Ezekiel xxxvi.25–28, with its reference to cleansing with clean water, and Hebrews x.19–25, which speaks of 'our bodies washed with pure water'. The body is then clothed in white vestments, a small censer is placed in the right hand and a napkin containing grains of incense in the left, and a cross and a book of the gospels are placed under the arms. A hymn, alleluias, psalm and gospel (John xviii.1–11) are followed by a prayer that all present may be made worthy of the washing of Christ in the upper room, by the washing of their hearts through repentance and by the washing of their bodies in the holiness of the font of baptism. A canticle, hymn, litany, and further prayer concludes this part of the rite.

Two canons then follow, the first being said in the house, and the second at the door. The body is then carried to the church, where at the entrance to the porch a further canon is said, and another actually in the porch. When the body is taken inside the church it is first placed in front of the cross, then in front of the *bema*, and finally in front of the altar, and a canon is said at each of these places. When the body has been laid in front of the altar, Psalm xxiii is recited, and the anointing of the dead then takes place, as described in the following rubric:

> And the priest takes the holy *muron*, and pours it out first on the forehead, as the holy Dionysius of Athens, a disciple of St Paul the Apostle, enjoins. For he expounds in order the mystery, which let no one in such a grade and order of Christianity as this contaminate with heathen abominations. For such is the apostolic canon.[13]

The priests present are then instructed to kiss the altar, tabernacle, sanctuary, and the gospel-book in the arms of the departed, saying as they do so the *Sharakan* of salutation.

> Hail to thee, holy church. Hail to thee, altar of holiness. Hail to you, ranks of the priesthood. I have set forth again on the road to the creator of heaven.

The body is then taken from the *bema* into the nave of the church, where the congregation bestows the last kiss. It is then carried to the door, where a canon is said, and after that to the four sides of the 'tabernacle'—presumably either the tomb, or the church itself. On the east, south, and west sides a psalm is recited and a lesson is read; on the north side a full canon is recited. The body is then placed in the tomb, two further lessons are read, and a prayer is then recited, followed by an exhortation described as the 'Rest of the blessed John, the evangelist of our Lord Jesus Christ'. After this the grave is filled in. The concluding section of the rite consists of a hymn, the *Gloria in excelsis*, responses, a lesson, a prayer for the 'sealing of the tomb' (ascribed to St Basil), further responses, a hymn, and a prayer. It is noteworthy that there is scarcely any overlap between the prayers of this rite for the burial of clergy and the funeral service for laymen, though both offices are marked by prayers of extreme verbosity.

The Coptic Order

By contrast the burial offices of the Coptic church are considerably simpler in character, though they offer many more variations for different categories of persons; variations, however, which only consist in the provision of different psalms and lessons, and a special prayer appropriate to the rank of the departed person. According to Burmester's description of contemporary Coptic practice,[14] as soon as death has occurred the eyes and mouth of the person are closed, and the body is washed and clothed in new garments, an ecclesiastic being robed in the vestments appropriate to his order. The body is then placed in the coffin, with its hands crossed over the breast, and four candles are lit round about it. If the departed is an ecclesiastic, psalms and hymns are recited for so long as the body remains in the house. When the priest arrives for the beginning of the funeral service, he recites a prayer of thanksgiving, and if there is a choir present, 'Remember me, O Lord, when thou comest into thy kingdom' together with the *Trisagion*, words which are repeated on arrival at the church.

In the church the office begins with the prayer of thanksgiving, followed by the prayer of incense, the *Gloria* and the Lord's Prayer. Psalm li is then recited, followed by a number of short extracts from psalms, each concluding with an Alleluia (Psalms cxxxix.7–10; cxix.175–6; cxv.16–18) and finally Psalm cxvi. The priest then proclaims 'Bless me. Behold repentance. Forgive me, my fathers and my brethren. Pray for me', to which the choir responds with the Gloria. The 'prayer of incense of Paul' is then said, as in the Liturgy, and this is followed by the reading of the Epistle (I Corinthians xv.1–23). Again, as in the Liturgy, the *Trisagion* and the prayer of the Gospel are said, and the Gospel (John v,19–29) is read. After the Gospel the order parallels that of the Coptic *synaxis*, with the 'three great prayers', for peace, for the patriarch and clergy, and for the faithful, and after these the Creed is said. The burial prayer, 'O God eternal, who knowest the hidden things before they are', is then recited by the priest, followed by the Lord's Prayer, at the conclusion of which the priest is directed to give 'the Absolution of the Son', a prayer for forgiveness addressed to Christ, which occurs in the *Enarxis* of the Coptic Liturgy.[15] A prayer for the safe journey of the departed to paradise then follows:

> Master, Lord God, the Almighty, Father of our Lord and our God and our Saviour, Jesus Christ, we pray and beseech thy goodness, Lover of man, on behalf of thy servant, *N*, who has gone forth from the body, that thou mayest send unto him an angel of mercy, an angel of righteousness, an angel of peace, that they may bring him to thee without fear. All his impieties of tongue, all his transgressions, forgive him. Let the guardians of the door, the fearful speakers, flee from before him. Let the counsel of the Adversary be destroyed. Let the wrath of the dragon be in vain. Let the mouths of the lions be shut. Let the evil spirits be dispersed. Let the Gehenna of fire be quenched. Let the sleepless worm be still. Let the changing darkness be enlightened. Let the angels of light walk before him. Let the gate of righteousness be open unto him. Let him become a partaker in the choir of the heavenly ones. Bring him into the paradise of delight. Feed him from the tree of life. Cause him to recline in the bosom of our forefathers, Abraham, Isaac, and Jacob, in thy kingdom. We also entreat of him in this place that he also may remember us before thee, through the grace and the compassion and the love of men of thine only-begotten Son, our Lord and our God, and our Saviour Jesus Christ, through whom, &c.

According to the rubrics this prayer is to be said over the grave, but Burmester notes that in practice it is now said in the church. It is interesting that a prayer which so strongly plays on the imagery of the journey of the soul after death should occur in an Egyptian service, knowing how important a part the voyage of the dead played in ancient Egyptian religion. The service in church concludes with a further prayer of absolution and the Blessing. At the grave there is a short committal. The choir sings 'Remember me, O Lord, when thou comest into thy kingdom', and the Lord's prayer is then said by all, after which the priest greets the mourners. In Holy Week, because neither prayers for the dead nor the use of incense is customary, the burial office consists only of an Old Testament lesson, a psalm, versicle, and Gospel. A memorial service for those dying during Holy Week is held after the Liturgy on Palm Sunday.

On the third day after death the service known as 'the lifting of the mat' takes place at the house of the departed, and this service is again held on the fortieth day after his death, but on this occasion it takes place in the church. The curious name of the service is a reference to the former custom of removing the mats on which the mourners sat three days after the death occurred. It may well be that it is this practice which is indicated in canon xxxiii of Hippolytus, which speaks of the ἀνάλημψις made for the dead.[16] The service itself follows the pattern of the burial office, with different psalmody and lessons, and concludes after the Creed with a prayer for the departed and for the consolation of the mourners, the Lord's Prayer, absolution and blessing.

The Ethiopian Order

The Ethiopian liturgy of burial is contained in the *Metshafe Ginzet*. At the house of the departed the body is washed and prepared for burial, whilst the psalms, the gospel of John, and the 'praises of Mary' are said, followed by further prayers and psalmody. As in the other Eastern rites Psalm cxix is appointed for the funeral procession, being said in seven sections on each occasion when the bearers halt. Thus the need for the bearers to rest is given liturgical significance. In the church the liturgy is celebrated—the body of a priest or deacon being taken into the sanctuary, and the body of a layman being placed before the sanctuary entrance. At the conclusion of the liturgy the farewell kiss is given, and the body is anointed with oil. Further psalmody and the 'praises of Mary' are appointed for the burial.[17] The body is buried so that the head, if raised, would look east in preparation for the Second Coming.[18]

Ginzet, which as it now stands is dated by Harden from the end of the thirteenth and the beginning of the fourteenth century,[19] reflects the pattern of burial custom described in the Ethiopic version of the *Didascalia*, a text which lies behind a large part of the *Apostolic Constitutions*. In this the writer instructs the faithful in the following way:

> Gather yourselves together diligently in the church and read the holy Scripture, over those righteous Christians who have fallen asleep, and your brethren the martyrs who have entered into rest in the faith of Christ; and celebrate for them the thanksgiving of the oblation, (and) offer in the church his holy Body and precious Blood. And when you bring (them) to the church and to the tomb, sing psalms over them, for (it is said) 'precious in the sight of the Lord is the death of the righteous'.[20]

43

Prayer for the dead appears specifically in *Ginzet* in the prayer of *fithat* (loosing), which is said both at the house of the deceased and just before entering the church. Cowley gives the following excerpt from this prayer:

> O God . . . we praise and bless thee and pray for the soul of thy servant *N*. Have mercy on him according to thy plentiful grace. For by thy baptism thou didst work forgiveness for those baptised likewise in the true faith. O Lord, forgive thy servant, because of thy blood of the New Covenant, in which thou gavest us forgiveness, mercy and salvation for eternity.[21]

Because the final decision is not made about the departed until the Last Judgment, it is possible to pray for all the departed, including the saints, and some of the anaphoras of the Ethiopian Liturgy contain petitions for the departed. A good example is from the *Anaphora of St Athanasius:*

> We pray thee, O Lord, and entreat thee for those who have fallen asleep, our fathers and our brethren who have passed from this world, that thou wouldest give them a peaceful rest . . . And those also whose names we know not, remember thou them in thy mercy and write their names in the book of life in Jerusalem.[22]

Tezkar (remembrance of the dead, by the giving of alms to priests and deacons to pray for the departed) is encouraged.[23]

Ethiopian burial practice can also include the winding of a strip of parchment, inscribed with a mixture of prayers and magical formulae, around the body. This is known as the *Lefafa Tsedek*, or 'Bandlet of righteousness', and although, as Budge comments in his translation of the text, the present form does not date back earlier than the sixteenth century, the ideas expressed in it are much older. Ethiopian tradition holds that the *Lefafa Tsedek* was given by Christ to Mary for use as a kind of safe-conduct or passport for the departed on his perilous journey after death.

> Whosoever hath gotten possession of this book, shall neither descend into the place of torment nor into Sî'ôl . . . Whoever shall carry it, and whoever shall attach (or hang) it to his neck (or body), his sins shall be remitted to him. And if he repeateth it with his voice at the time of the Offering (his sins) shall be remitted to him, and he shall be cleansed from the pollution of sin. And if they (i.e. the priests) shall make at the bier (or tomb) the sign of the seal of SOLOMON thrice with this book, after he is buried, the angels shall conduct him through the gates of life. And they shall make him to arrive before God, and shall introduce him into the kingdom of heaven.[24]

The text contains a prayer for the journey after death, in which the theme of the angelic guides again appears.

> Protect thou me, O Christ, so that the angels of darkness may not obstruct my soul. And let there be sent unto me the angels of light, Michael and Gabriel—those august angels—and the Paraclete, and the Spirit of Righteousness, so that the angels of darkness may never obstruct my soul, and that the Lord may not make me to stand in the darkness (amid) the gnashing of teeth.[25]

The Syrian Orders

The Syrian burial services of the Assyrians and Chaldeans, the Syrian Jacobites and the Maronites all have close similarities. The services are generally known by titles indicating that they are concerned with the departure of the Christian from this world to the next, and the texts contain numerous prayers concerned with the journey beyond the grave and written as though spoken by the person departed. Because a funeral is a taking leave of the world it was customary for lay people to be carried from their own houses to the place of burial, because their house was where they lived and belonged, whereas priests and monks, who were specially bound to the church, were taken first to the church and then to the place of burial.[26] This is still the case in the Assyrian and Chaldean tradition, but Maronite practice has now been modified and laymen are taken to the church as well as priests and monks. Modern transport has likewise modified the use of the lengthy chants provided for the funeral processions, and the chants are either anticipated by being included in the service at the house of the departed, or are omitted altogether.

The Assyrian Order

The eastern Syrian tradition of the Assyrians (and the Chaldean Uniates) can be traced back at least as far as the twelfth century in its present form, and much of the order is clearly earlier, some of the funeral chants being known from a ninth-century manuscript (Vat. Syr. 92) in which they are attributed to St Ephraem. The order falls into four sections: (1) the washing and preparation of the body; (2) the vigil of prayer; (3) the funeral procession; and (4) the burial proper. G. P. Badger, in his classic work *The Nestorians and their Rituals* (1852), provides the text of the fullest of these rites, the *Kahneita*, or the burial service for priests.[27] There are variations for the burial of lay men and women, children under seven, and deacons.

The ritual of the washing of the body has been seen as bearing a close resemblance to Jewish practice.[28] It begins with the turning of the face of the departed to the east, and making the sign of the cross on the forehead.[29] The body is then washed, beginning with the head, face, and neck, then the right and left forearms, and the right and left sides, and then the remainder of the body. When the washing is finished the body is clothed in white garments 'as in the days of his wedding'. The washing may take place 'in the house of the departed, or upon the roofs, or, if they have no place, in the church', and whilst it is being carried out the '*Moutwa* of the washing' is recited. The *Moutwa* is the equivalent of the Greek *kathisma*, and consists of a group of verses from the psalms, followed by an anthem. Before the *Moutwa*, a short introductory section is read. This begins with an invocatory prayer—'Let us thank, worship, and praise the hidden and adorable power of thy glorious Trinity, for thou art the Lord of the two worlds which thou hast created, O Lord of our death and life, Father, Son, and Holy Ghost. Amen.'—which is followed by Psalm xx.1–5, then by a second prayer and Psalm xliii. Incense is offered, and a further prayer is said. At the end of the first *Moutwa* the priest prays that the Lord who had mercy on the penitent thief will also have mercy on the departed, and recites the first six verses of Psalm cxvi. This is followed by the *Akkapta*, a short, linking anthem, whose words are: 'Thy good Spirit shall lead me in the way of life. O thou who quickenest the dead, glory be to thee.' Two short concluding prayers follow:

> Glory to thy sweet-sounding voice, and to thy sovereign word, which in thy grace and mercy shall summon us from the grave, and gather together our dust from every quarter, and shall make us a new creation, O Lord of our death and life, Father, Son, and Holy Ghost. Amen.

> Blessed art thou upon earth, and praised art thou in heaven, O thou who art the cause of our life, and the righteous hope of our souls, O Lord of our death and life, Father, Son and Holy Ghost. Amen.

Four other *Moutwas*, constructed on the same pattern, follow, in between which hymns are sung. An example is given below.

The Lord whose cross thou hast confessed, may he give rest to thy soul, O our brother; and when he shall come in his great glory, may he give thee bliss in his kingdom.

Depart in peace, O our brother, the Lord accompany thee, and the cherub who keepeth the door of paradise open the gate thereof before thee.

By the ministry in which I served with you, let not my remembrance be forgotten from among you, and when you stand in the sanctuary think of me in your prayers.[30]

When the five *moutwas* are finished, the funeral procession is formed, and the '*qalê* of the way' (Processional chant) is begun:

From this time forth and for ever. My harp is turned into mourning, and my lute into the voice of them that weep. Abide in peace, O temporary dwelling-place which canst not deliver those who possess thee; I am now going to a region of light, the abode of the righteous, who have ceased from their labours.

The *qalê* is constructed on the same principles as the *moutwas*, verses of psalms followed by short anthems. In the case of laymen it is merely stated that 'when they go out from the village, they put the bier in a pure place, and they perform fully three '*ûnîn* (anthems)', but the bodies of priests are taken into the church, where there are prayers and a celebration of the eucharist.[31] There are four Scripture readings at the beginning of this section of the rite: Numbers xx.22–29; Acts xx.17–38; I Corinthians xv.34–38; and John v.19–30. The deacon then begins the litany:

Let us all stand in sorrow and sadness, and let us say: Lord have mercy upon us. O God, the Father of Spirits, and the Lord of all those who are in the body; we pray thee to have mercy upon us.

Two prayers for the departed follow this litany, the second of which is of some interest for the curious use which it makes of numerical references.

When this one world shall be dissolved, and the two lights shall be extinguished, and the three trumpets shall sound, and the four winds shall cease to blow, and the five senses shall fail, and the six days shall flow into one day, and the seven thousand years shall come to an end, and the eight tones of music shall sound and shout aloud, and the nine circles of the angels shall be amazed, and the ten commandments shall be enquired of, and the eleven Apostles with him to whom the ministry fell by lot shall sit upon thrones, and the twelve tribes of Israel shall be judged, and the righteous shall inherit light, but the wicked shall be confounded—in that bitter and awful hour, fit this thy servant, O Lord, to hear the welcome voice: Come, thou good and faithful servant, enter into the joy of thy Lord; O Lord of all, Father, Son, and Holy Ghost. Amen.

A short prayer praising the mercies of God is said, and after this the anthem of the *Bema* is sung, whilst the people communicate. There are then two prayers, that the sacraments of which the people have partaken may avail to them for the forgiveness of their sins, and a prayer of thanksgiving. This concludes the service in church.

As the body is carried from the church an anthem is sung, beginning, 'Abide in peace, O Church, for I am going away, and let those who dwell in thee in righteousness pray for me', followed by up to ten *ûnîn* recited in the courtyard of the church. When these are completed the procession to the grave is formed and the '*qalê* of the approach' is begun: '*I was glad when they said unto me, Let us go up to the house of the Lord.* The Lord shall come to raise up the departed, and to fulfil the hope of the dead.' On arrival at the grave, the bier is placed beside the grave whilst the deacon says a short litany, that God may guide the departed to the haven of the righteous, write his name in the book of life, and number him with the elect, which is followed by two prayers, the second of which is as follows:

> Blessed is the mighty decree of thy Majesty which killeth and maketh alive, which bringeth down to *Sheol* and raiseth up, and which clotheth our bodies with glory in the resurrection, O Lord of our death and life, Father, Son, and Holy Ghost. Amen.

Then whilst an anthem is sung, the last farewell is made, which, according to Badger, is done by touching the hands of the departed with both hands and raising them to the lips, in the same way as the kiss of peace is given in the East Syrian tradition.[32] During the recitation of a further anthem the body is placed in the grave, and the priest, after praying that the departed may share in the resurrection, and may be judged righteous in the day of judgment, casts earth upon the body. According to Badger this is scattered in the form of a cross, but the brief account of the ritual of washing the dead expressly forbids this: 'the priest throws a little dust in the grave, but not in the form of a cross, as foolish people do'.[33] The grave is then filled in, and three final prayers are said.

The day after burial a service of consolation is said at the grave, beginning, in the case of priests with a prayer acknowledging the justice and mercy of God, followed by Psalm xxvi. This is followed by an anthem celebrating the faith of the one departed, and praying that God will not forget him. A prayer for those who mourn is then said, together with a second prayer for mercy and forgiveness. Psalm lxvii is then recited, followed by two anthems, the *Trisagion*, and further prayers. The office concludes with an anthem on the theme of the universality of death, which comes to all men, whether they be the faithful of the Old Testament or the wealthy and powerful.

> Ask of *Sheol* and she will tell you where they are: ask of the earth and she will show you the place of their burial.
>
> They all are embosomed in the ground, and there shall they remain till the resurrection-day.
>
> One decree shall go forth to the four quarters of the world, and shall gather together and separate the dust of man from the dust of the earth.
>
> One decree shall shake the earth, the mother of the dead, and they shall rise from the dead and sing praises.
>
> Whilst there is space for repentance let us labour a little, and now that the door of mercy is open let us pray for mercy.

The Maronite Order

An analysis of the earliest surviving manuscript of the Maronite funeral liturgy has recently been published by J. Azzi.[34] This manuscript (Vat. Syr. 59) dates from 1266 and contains two offices, that for bishops, priests, and deacons, and that for monks. Azzi's work concerns the second of these two orders, but Jean Tabet in his unpublished notes on the Eastern Office of the dead considers the former as well.[35] The two orders differ mainly in the readings and chants prescribed: the basic structure is similar and can be set out briefly in tabular form.

I. *Introductory office in house (or monastic cell) of the departed*
   (a) Psalmody (not in monastic office)
   (b) *Hussoyo* (office of incense)
   (c) *Mazmura*—threefold farewell chant (for clergy)
       or *Qōlo*—hymn (in the monastic office)

II. *Procession to the Church*
   (a) Processional chant
   (b) Entrance chant

III. *Service in Church*
  (a) Three-fold *tesmesto*—service of psalmody and chants (for clergy), single office of psalmody (psalms ciii, cxxx, and lxiii) and prayer (for monks)
  (b) Biblical readings interspersed with chants (25 readings for clergy; 22 for monks, the majority in each case being taken from the Old Testament)
  (c) Office of incense (not in monastic office)
  (d) Farewell to the altar (not in monastic office)
  (e) Rite of the peace—farewell to the community (not in office for the clergy)
  (f) Farewell to the Church and procession to the place of burial

IV. *The burial*
  (a) Anointing of the body (in office for the clergy only)
  (b) Placing in the tomb
  (c) Final prayer

The many chants in these offices have as their theme either the plight of the departed setting out on the journey of death and leaving this world behind, or God as Lord of life and death as seen in the deaths of the faithful in the Old Testament. The chants are very often written as though in the person of the departed, and some are constructed as dialogues between the departed and the congregation who have assembled to bid him farewell. Some examples will illustrate the characteristic imagery and ideas. The righteous desire to be with Abraham, but to reach it the departed must cross the sea of fire to where Abraham keeps the door:

> It is terrible, the place where I am come, and full of danger. For there is there a sea of fire which all humanity must cross. At the crossing Abraham stands, and at his side the righteous man. Give me your hand, O righteous one, that I may come to you. And when I shall come, I shall cry out: 'Glory to you, Lord'.[36]

Or again, a chant with the theme of the eucharist as the medicine of immortality:

> I have borne you, O Son of God, as a viaticum for the exodus. I have eaten your holy body, that the fire may not devour me. And because I have placed it on my eyes, may they see your mercy. I was no stranger to you, Lord, in this age, that I may be cast out in the other. Do not place me at the side of the goats, but vouchsafe to admit me among the lambs, at your right hand, to praise you.[37]

The reference to the placing of the eucharistic bread on the eyes in this chant would seem to reflect the tradition recorded by Cyril of Jerusalem that communicants touched their eyes with the consecrated bread before partaking of communion: 'Carefully hallow your eyes by the touch of the sacred Body, and then partake, taking care to lose no part of it.'[38] As an example of a dialogue chant *Qōlo 'Abo Mrahmono'*, which occurs after the twenty-first reading in the burial office for clergy, may be cited.

Congregation: Lord, give rest, life, and happiness to our father, in the kingdom with all the righteous who have loved you, believed in you, and kept your commandments.

Departed: My brothers, remember and celebrate my memorial, that the remembrance of me may not disappear from among you, seeing that I am separated from you for ever in order that I may live for my Lord and my God.

Congregation: Console your conscience by the yoke of your will, for you have endured and won by the experience of your freedom, so that Christ will crown you with glory and make you worthy of his.

Departed: This is so, my well-beloved, but I trust that if, at his appearing, I reveal my secrets, I will rejoice because he will have pity on me at the day of his coming.[39]

This dialogue continues for another thirty or so stanzas.

The Maronite burial office of the laity is simpler than that for either clergy or religious, but has a very similar structure. The central section of psalmody and prayer is built around the three psalms, ciii, cxxx, and lxiii, as in the monastic office.

The Syrian Jacobite office, Tabet comments, is closely linked with both the Maronite and Chaldean offices, and likewise makes provision for numerous biblical readings in the orders for clergy and monks. Tabet notes that in the opening prayer of the order of lay burial there is reference to the departed contending against malevolent spirits, and in a parallel text in the Maronite order there is a petition for an angel of peace to guide and protect the departed soul through the domain of the evil spirits who inhabit the air. The final prayer of the Syrian Jacobite order is a version of the old Eastern prayer, 'God of the spirits and of all flesh.'[40]

*   *   *

The burial rites of the various traditions of Eastern Christianity are, as we have seen, characterized by lengthy prayers and anthems in a way which is not the case in the West. Very often a simple, original pattern can be discerned beneath the elaboration of anthems and prayers, which often tend to draw together a multiplicity of biblical images, and to preface petitions for the departed or the mourners with a lengthy rehearsal of the saving acts of God. All the rites witness to the way in which the actual requirements of burial, preparation of the body, the funeral procession, and the burial itself, were regarded as actions with which the church was intimately concerned, and for which liturgical provision was made, hence the long anthems provided for recitation during the washing and laying-out of the body, and the multiplicity of anthems, psalms, and readings for the funeral procession. The note of joy and triumph as characteristic of the Christian funeral, in which death in the hope of resurrection was seen as the completion of the Christian's baptismal life, is one which is still evident in the Eastern rites, with their Alleluias and their praise of the mercy and justice of God. Many of the prayers draw very heavily on the Old Testament for their phraseology, and it is often the Old Testament saints who are named as those with whom the faithful departed will be numbered. The biblical readings are overwhelmingly drawn from the Old Testament. These characteristics may point to an originally strong Jewish influence on these rites. Inevitably, because the Eastern rites of burial have been so little studied, the pattern of their historical development remains obscure, and much more detailed work will have to be done before a comprehensive picture of their evolution and relationship to each other can be constructed.

Seraphion

(Wisd. xvi.13)
(Numb. xvi, 22; I Sam. ii.6)
(Wisd. xvi.13)

God, who hast authority of life and death, God of the spirits and Master of all flesh, God who killest and makest alive, who bringest down to the gate of Hades, and bringest up, who createdst the spirit of man within him and takest to thyself the souls of the saints and givest rest, who alterest and changest, and transformest thy creature, as is right and expedient, being thyself alone incorruptible, unalterable, and eternal, we beseech thee for the repose and rest of this thy servant, give rest to his soul, his spirit in green places, in chambers of rest with Abraham, and Isaac, and Jacob, and all thy saints: and raise up his body in the day which thou hast ordained, according to thy promises which cannot lie, that thou mayest render to it also the heritage of which it is worthy in thy holy pasture. Remember not his transgressions and sins: and cause his going forth to be peaceable and blessed. Heal the griefs of those that pertain to him with the spirit of consolation: and grant unto us all a good end through thine only-begotten Jesus Christ through whom to thee (is) the glory and the strength in holy Spirit to the ages of ages. Amen.

(Psalm xxiii.2)

Apostolic Constitutions

O thou who art by nature immortal, and hast no end of thy being, from whom every creature, whether immortal or mortal, is derived; who didst make man a rational creature, the citizen of this world, in his constitution mortal, and didst add the promise of a resurrection: who didst not suffer Enoch and Elias to taste of death; the God of Abraham, the God of Isaac, and the God of Jacob and the God of them, not as of dead, but as of living persons: for the souls of all men live with thee, and the spirits of the righteous are in thy hand, which no torment can touch; for they are all sanctified under thy hand: do thou now also look upon this thy servant, whom thou hast selected and received into another state, and forgive him if voluntarily or involuntarily he has sinned, and afford him merciful angels, and place him in the bosom of the patriarchs and prophets and apostles, and of all those that have pleased thee from the beginning of the world, where there is no grief, sorrow, nor lamentation; but the peaceable region of the godly, and the undisturbed land of the upright, and of those that therein see the glory of thy Christ; by whom glory, honour, and worship, thanksgiving, and adoration be to thee in the Holy Spirit, for ever. Amen.

(Matt. xxii.34)
(Wisd. iii.1)

(Rev. xxi.4)

Comparative table of Eastern burial prayers—contd.

Greek (lay burial)

(Numb. xvi.22)

(Psalm. xxiii.2)

(Rev. xxi.4)

O God of spirits and of all flesh, who hast trampled down Death, and overthrown the Devil, and given life unto thy world: Do thou, the same Lord, give rest to the soul of thy departed servant *N*, in a place of brightness, a place of verdure, a place of repose, whence all sickness, sorrow, and sighing have fled away. Pardon every transgression which he hath committed, whether by word or deed or thought. For thou art a good God and lovest mankind; because there is no man who liveth and sinneth not: for thou only art without sin, and thy righteousness is to all eternity, and thy word is true. For thou art the Resurrection and the Life, and the Repose of thy departed servant *N*, O Christ, our God, and unto thee we ascribe glory, together with thy Father who is from everlasting, and thine all-holy and good and life-giving Spirit, now and ever, and unto ages of ages. Amen.

Greek (priestly burial)

(I Tim. vi.16)

(I Sam. ii.6)

O Master, Lord our God, who alone hast immortality, and dwellest in light unapproachable; who slayest and makest alive; who castest down into hell, and again raisest up; thou in wisdom hast created man, and returnest him to the earth again, exacting the spiritual debit: receive, we beseech thee, the soul of thy servant, and grant him rest in the bosom of Abraham and Isaac and Jacob; and give him the crown of thy righteousness, the portion of the saved, in the glory of thine elect. And for those things which in this world he hath wrought for thy Name's sake, may he receive a rich reward in the mansions of thy Saints; through the grace and bounties and love towards mankind of thine only-begotten Son, our Lord Jesus Christ.

Coptic

(Wisd. xvi.3)

O God eternal, who knowest the hidden things before they are, who didst bring all things into being out of nothing, in whose hands is the authority of life and death, who enterest into the gates of Amenti, and dost bring up. A mystery of thine is the creation of man, O Master, and the dissolution of thy temporal creation, and their eternal resurrection. To thee is rendered thanksgiving for all things, and for entry into the world, and for departures out of it in hopes of the resurrection. (We bless the coming of thy Christ, and the sonship thou hast given us in him, who condescended to our troubles and did raise us with himself into freedom from sufferings.) Receive, O Lord, in holy charge, this soul of thy servant N, and keep it in rest until the resurrection and the appearing of Christ, in the bosom of our holy fathers, Abraham and Isaac and Jacob, whence sorrow and trouble and sighing flee away. And if he have committed any sins against thee as man, forgive him and pardon him, and let all his chastisements pass away, for thou didst not form man unto destruction but unto life. And give him rest in that place; and on us, too, here have mercy, and make us worthy to serve thee with freedom from care. Them that survive console. Them that are troubled comfort. Them that are orphaned maintain. And them that are gathered together and share in their trouble—have mercy upon them and bless them. Give unto them an heavenly reward in the world to come and for ever and ever. For thou art a merciful God and pitiful, and unto thee we offer up glory and honour and worship, Father, Son, and Holy Ghost, now and ever. Amen.

(Numb. xvi.22)
(Rev. xxi.4)

(Rev. xxi.4)

Armenian

God of spirits and all bodies, who hast annihilated death and trampled upon Satan, and bestowed life upon the world; rest the spirit of this thy servant in a place of light, and in a place of repose, from which are far removed pain and sorrow and lamentation. And of all the sins which have been committed by him, whether in word or in deed or in thought, do thou, as thou art kindly and lovest mankind, bestow remission upon him by thy grace. For who is the man who shall live and not sin? Since thou alone art without sin, and thy kingdom is a kingdom for ever, and thy words are true. For thou art the life and resurrection of all that sleep; and to thee are due glory, rule, and honour, now and ever, and to eternity of eternities. Amen.

Comparative table of Eastern burial prayers—contd.

Liturgy of St James	Liturgy of the Syrian Jacobites
(Numb. xvi.22) Remember, also, O Lord, the God of the spirits of all flesh, those that we have not remembered of the orthodox (from righteous Abel unto this very day). Do thou thyself refresh them (in the land of the living, in thy kingdom, in the joy of paradise) in the bosoms of Abraham and Isaac and Jacob our holy fathers, (Rev. xxi.4) whence pain and grief and tribulation have fled away, where the light of Thy countenance surveyeth all things and shineth perpetually. (And grant us to make a christian end and to please thee, and direct our lives without sin and in peace, O Lord, Lord; and gather us together under the feet of thine elect when thou wilt, only that it be without shame and without iniquity).	(Numb. xvi.22) O Lord, Lord God of Spirits and of all flesh, remember, O Lord, those whom we have mentioned and those whom we have not mentioned, who have passed from this life in the orthodox faith. Rest their souls and bodies and spirits, deliver them from eternal punishment to come and vouchsafe to them delight in the bosom of Abraham and of Isaac and of Jacob, where the light of thy countenance visiteth, whence pains and tribulations and sighings are fled away. Impute to them none of their offences and enter not into (Psalm: cxiii.2) judgment with thy servants, for in thy sight shall no man living be justified: for there is no man that is not guilty of sin and that is pure from defilement of them that are among the sons of men upon the earth, save only our Lord and God and Saviour Jesus Christ, thine only-begotten Son, through whom we too hope to obtain mercies and forgiveness of sins for his sake, both for ourselves and for them.

4   *The medieval West*

As with the Eastern rites, so in the Western Church the origins and the development of the liturgy of burial remain comparatively unresearched. The actions involved in the preparation of the body for burial, its removal to the church, a service in church, and then a further procession to the place of burial followed by the burial itself provided the pattern around which particular liturgical forms grew up, but there was always a certain fluidity in the distribution of the prayers and psalmody which came to be used. Unlike the East, with its different rites for different categories of men and women within the church, in the West it was the varied rites of the different monastic orders which emerged during the medieval period which contributed to the development of different traditions and the growth of more complex and elaborate rites. It is difficult at present to establish any precise account of the detailed development of the liturgy of burial because so much still requires to be done in the way of critical analysis of texts. Moreover, as Philippeau points out, the frequent placing of the burial liturgy at the end of service books, and the inevitable exposure of the books to the elements during funeral processions and the committal in the churchyard, have led to the burial rite being absent in many cases from otherwise complete sacramentaries.[1] The account which follows can therefore only be a tentative and general survey of medieval developments.

One of the earliest Roman rites was published by Andrieu as *Ordo* XLIX of his medieval *Ordines Romani*.[2] This text is that of an eleventh century manuscript (Vat. Lib. Cod. Ottobon. 312), but the rite itself is considerably older. This is shown by its close resemblance to the sequence of prayers headed *Incipit de migratione animae* found in a manuscript of the Gelasian sacramentary thought to have been transcribed *c.* 800.[3]

The prayers of this Gelasian order commence with the reading of the Passion according to St John at the bedside of the dying man, followed by the recitation of Psalm xlii, *Quemadmodum*, with the antiphon *Tu iussisti* ('Lord, you commanded that I should be born, you have promised that I shall be raised up; your command has come that I entrust my body to the earth; the soul which you have given me, receive, O God.'). Then, after a litany and a prayer (words unspecified) the dying man is given his Viaticum. As soon as death has occurred the antiphon *Subvenite sancti Dei;* Psalm cxiv, *In exitu Israel*, with its paschal and baptismal overtones, with the antiphon *Suscipiat te;* and the antiphon *Chorus angelorum* are recited. The body is then washed and clothed in vesture appropriate to the rank of the deceased, and laid on the bier, during which psalms are continuously recited, concluding with Psalm xciii, *Dominus regnavit*, with the antiphon *De terra formasti me*. The body is then borne in procession to the church whilst further psalms are chanted (Psalm cxvi, *Dilexi quoniam*, with antiphon *Audivi vocem de caelo*, and Psalm xliii, *Domine exaudi*). At the entrance to the church the antiphon *Aperite mihi portas* is said. The rite abruptly concludes with the statement that the body is carried into the church preceded by a cross and lighted candles whilst the antiphons of the burial office are sung.

Ordo XLIX contains much of the material found in this Gelasian rite, but· in a different order and with a number of additions. After the dying man has received his Viaticum the narrative of the passion is read by either priests or deacons at his bedside: no particular gospel is specified. As soon as the last breath has been drawn the responses *Subvenite sancti Dei* and *Suscipiat te Christus* are said followed by Psalm cxiv, *In exitu Israel*, with the antiphon *Chorus angelorum te suscipiat*. The priest is then directed to say the prayer appointed in the sacramentary, but the text is not given. They then proceed to the washing of the body, and the placing of it upon the bier. When this has been completed, and before leaving the house, Psalm xciii, *Dominus regnavit*, with the antiphon *De terra formasti me* is recited. The two rubrics which follow give the psalms and antiphons which are to be said after the body has been brought inside the church, and whilst it is being carried to burial, in that order. These are Psalm xlii, *Quemadmodum* (Antiphon: *Tu iussisti nasci me Domine*) and Psalm iv, *Cum invocarem* (Antiphon: *In paradisum deducant te angeli*) in the church; and, for the funeral procession, Psalm xv, *Domine quis habitavit* (Antiphon: *Qui posuit animam tuam ad vitam*); Psalm li, *Miserere*, (Antiphon: *Animam de corpore* ('Lord, make the soul which you have taken away from the body to rejoice with your saints in glory')); Psalm xxv, *Ad te Domine levavi* (Antiphon: *Vivi Domine* ('Lord you see my lowliness and my suffering, forgive all my sins!')); Psalm lvi (?), *Miserere mei Deus* (Antiphon: *In regnum Dei deducant te angeli*). The final rubric states that when the body is placed in the church, all present pray for the soul of the departed until the burial itself takes place, the prayers consisting of psalms, responses, a mass, or lessons from the book of Job. When the hour of the vigil service comes, the psalms are directed to be said without Alleluia, and the priest is then directed to say a prayer (unspecified) whilst Psalm cxviii, *Confitemini Domino*, is sung with the antiphon *Aperite mihi portas iustitiae*, 'Open to me the gates of righteousness, that entering into them I may confess the Lord' (Psalm cxviii. 19). At this point the service of *Ordo* XLIX ends.

It is clear that both this rite, and the Gelasian rite in MS Berlin Phillipps 1667, are incomplete, for no account is given in either of them of the burial proper. Frank, in his study of early Roman *Ordines Defunctorum*, draws attention to this, and suggests that a full text of the rite is to be found in a Cologne manuscript (No. 123), a text which is supported in many details by the eighth- or ninth-century manuscript of the Gelasian sacramentary, originating probably from northern Gaul, known as Rheinau 30.[4] The Cologne rite is headed *Ordo defunctorum qualiter agatur erga defunctum a morte detentum* and follows closely the pattern of *Ordo* XLIX: Viaticum; the reading of the Passion; and psalmody and responses immediately after the moment of death. The Psalms and responses are not quite the same as those in *Ordo* XLIX: *Requiem aeternam* is to be said in response to *Subvenite sancti Dei*, and *Suscipiat te Christus* is given as the antiphon for Psalm cxiv, *In exitu Israel*. The antiphon which follows, *Chorus angelorum*, is itself succeeded in the Cologne manuscript by Psalm cxvi, *Dilexi quoniam*, and then the priest's prayer as in *Ordo* XLIX. After the washing of the body and the placing of it upon the bier have been carried out, the antiphon *De terra formasti me* is said, as in *Ordo* XLIX (Rheinau 30 has *Ad aeternam formasti me*), but the psalm which follows is not Psalm xciii, but Psalm xxiii, *Dominus regit me*. This is also the case in the Rheinau manuscript. The funeral procession is then formed and moves to the church singing psalms and antiphons, first Psalm xlii, *Quemadmodum*, with antiphon *Tu iussisti*, as in *Ordo* XLIX; then Psalm cxliii, *Domine exaudi*, as in MS Berlin Phillipps 1667, which differs here from *Ordo* XLIX. The Cologne manuscript, however, gives a different antiphon, *Audivi vocem*, in place of *Haec dies mortalis*. The four psalms, (xv, li, xxv, and (?) lvi) which then follow in *Ordo* XLIX are not found in the Cologne manuscript which moves straight to the rubric providing for the recitation of psalms (*psalmos vel responsoria permixtos*); readings from Job; the recitation of the psalms of the Vigil, without Alleluia; and for the body remaining in church until such time as a mass is celebrated for the soul of the departed. When all these things have been done, a second procession is formed and the body is carried to the grave preceded by lights and incense, whilst Psalm cxviii, *Confitemini Domino*, with the antiphon *Aperite mihi portas iustitiae* is sung. The Rheinau manuscript inserts the Gallican prayer *Deus universorum Creator* after the Mass, and also differs in its psalmody, prescribing Psalm xxv, *Ad te Domine levavi*, with the antiphon *In paradisum* and Psalm xlii, *Quemadmodum*, with the antiphon *Ingrediar in locum tabernaculum* at this point. The Cologne rite continues with the body being placed in the grave whilst the priest says the prayer, 'as it is set out in the sacramentary.' Psalms and antiphons are sung as follows: Psalm xlii, *Quemadmodum* (Antiphon: *Sitivit anima mea*); Psalm xliii, *Iudica me, Deus* (Antiphon: *Ingrediar in locum tabernaculi*); Psalm cxxxii, *Memento, Domine, David* (Antiphon: *Haec requires mea in saeculum saeculi hic habitabo quoniam elegi esse*). Rheinau again has a different order. All present are directed to pray for the soul of the departed and to sing the *Miserere*, whilst the priest says the burial preface *Debitum humani corporis sepeliendi officium*. The rite concludes with Psalm cxviii, *Confitemini Domino*, and the antiphon *Aperite mihi*.

In his comparison of these early rites Frank makes a number of points worthy of note. He observes that Rheinau 30 does not mention the Vigil office for the dead, though it is referred to in the Cologne order and in *Ordo* XLIX. He suggests that it is the Rheinau manuscript which is the more original at this point, and that the office of the dead was not originally a constituent part of the burial rite, though it became so quite early in the history of the Roman liturgy of burial. The *Instructio ecclesiastici ordinis*, for instance, which was edited by a Benedictine monk, *c.* 750–775, refers to the omission of Alleluia in the antiphons and responses to the psalms and lessons in the offices of the dead—both the vigil office and mattins.[5] Again, Frank notes that two of the psalms (xlii and cxviii) belonging to the burial proper have Easter associations in early liturgical use, and the effect of the appearance of the *Miserere* in the Rheinau text is to give it a more penitential character, the beginning of a development which continued throughout the medieval period.[6]

One of Frank's reasons for suspecting that *Ordo* XLIX does not provide us with the earliest text of the Roman burial rite is the appearance in it of the antiphon *In paradisum*. This occurs in different places in *Ordo* XLIX (the procession from the house to the church) and Rheinau 30 (the procession from the church to the place of burial) but it does not appear at all in the Cologne rite. Dom Capelle, who made an extensive examination of the history of the anthem, concluded that it was of Gallican provenance, but was likely to have been derived from an anthem in the Ambrosian rite of North Italy. In this rite the antiphon to Psalm lxi, *Exaudi Deus*, the seventh of the fourteen psalms appointed to be recited during the washing of the body, is what appears to be an adaptation of Psalm lxxiii. 23: *In consilium tuum deduces me, et postea in gloria suscipies me*. Capelle then suggested, on the basis of texts in the Fulda Sacramentary (tenth century) and Hartker (St Gall Codex, twelfth century), that the probable development of the text of the anthem was as follows:

Ambrosian: In paradisum deducant te angeli
            Et cum gloria suscipiant te sci martyres Dei
            (3 manuscripts have *cum gaudio*).
Fulda: In paradysum deducant te angeli
            Et cum gaudio suscipiant te martyres
            Perducant te in civitatem sanctam Hierusalem.
Hartker: In paradysum deducant te angeli
            In tuo adventu suscipiant te martyres
            Et perducant te in civitatem sanctam Hierusalem.

The *cum gaudio* of the Fulda text, Capelle suggested, would fit with the preceding rubric that lights and incense are born before the body with the singing of antiphons and psalms.[7]

The early burial rites which we have examined do not provide us with more than the occasional introductory phrase of the prayers to be used in the liturgy of burial, though they do give full account of the psalmody and antiphons. For the texts of the prayers we have to turn to the sacramentaries, where they are grouped according to the various stages of the burial rite: (1) commendatory prayers immediately after death has occurred; (2) the washing of the body; (3) before the body is carried to the grave; (4) at the grave before burial; (5) after burial and the final commendation. Not all of these titles are used in every one of the major manuscripts, but the pattern is common to them all.

The Gelasian burial prayers,[8] for instance, begin with a group of eight prayers headed 'Prayers after a man's death'. The first of these is the prayer *Pio recordationis affectu*, in which the departed is commemorated and God is asked to grant him rest and forgiveness. These themes are taken up in the following prayers, which petition that God will receive the soul of his servant 'coming back out of Egypt'; that God will send his angels to guide the departed soul in the way of righteousness; that the departed may be clothed in heavenly garments and washed in the sacred fountain of eternal life; and that he may be brought to share in the worship and joy of heaven with the patriarchs, prophets and martyrs, being granted the reward of *requiem et regnum*, the heavenly Jerusalem, and being found worthy of a place in the bosom of Abraham, Isaac, and Jacob. This section ends with the rubric that the chapter *In memoria aeterna* is said.

The second group of prayers are four appointed to be said before the body is carried to the grave. The first entreats God as the Judge of all and Lord of heaven and earth and of the dead, asking that he will count the spirit of the departed worthy of a place of rest and will grant him a share in the first resurrection. The second prayer repeats the request that the departed will be granted a place of refreshment, light, and peace, and will enjoy the fellowship of the saints. The final two prayers reaffirm these petitions and again ask that the departed may be granted a place in the bosom of the patriarchs and set free from the bonds of the body. In the third group of prayers, 'Prayers at the grave before burial', the same themes occur. The second prayer, *Opus misericordiae tuae est*, echoes in part the fourth prayer at the death bed, *Suscipe, Domine, animam servi tui*, with its petition for the angelic guidance of the departed soul. The latter prayer asks that Michael, the angel of God's last will (*tui testamenti*) may defend the departed,[9] and that he may be delivered from the powers of darkness and the places of punishment. There are three further prayers after the burial has taken place: that the body buried in weakness may be raised in power to take its place amongst the saints; and that the soul of the departed may be kept by God's mercy from the pains of hell and enter into the joy of heaven. The rites concludes with two prayers of commendation: *Commendamus tibi, Domine*, and *Deus apud quem omnia morientia vivunt*.

This was the form of burial service which was in use in France at the beginning of the eighth century. It was modified in the revision initiated by Peppin, the father of Charlemagne, from which emerged the texts partially reformed on a Roman model which have become known as the 'Gelasian of the eighth century'. As far as the burial liturgy was concerned the change largely involved the adding of further material at the beginning of the rite. The Sacramentary of Gellone, which is considered the best representative of the Gelasian of the eighth century, has an opening section headed 'Prayers over one departed, or the commendation of the soul'. This begins with the solemn commendation, *Proficiscere anima*, followed by a second prayer, *Deus ante cuius conspectum defertur*, the concluding prayer of the Gelasian rite, *Deus apud quem omnia morientia vivunt*, and the third prayer of the first section of the Gelasian, *Tu nobis Domine auxilium*, after which follow five *capitula*. In the Sacramentary of Gellone the opening section of the Gelasian prayers is specifically assigned to cover the washing of the body. The prayers given in MS Rheinau 30 are fewer in number but follow the same general pattern.[10] It is these two texts, Gellone and Rheinau 30, which provide us with the earliest attestation of the commendation *Proficiscere*, which is thought to have been derived from Benedictine sources. Despite its occurrence in these early texts, it did not become widely used until the twelfth century.[11]

When we turn to Alcuin's supplement to the *Hadrianum* (the Sacramentary sent to Charlemagne in 785 as a supposedly unadulterated version of the Gregorian Sacramentary) we find a radical revision of these earlier burial rites. Alcuin provides eight prayers for the commendation of the soul followed by psalmody. Of these eight only one is derived from the Gelasian: the opening prayer *Pio recordationis affectu*. The seven prayers which follow consist of four taken from Mozarabic sources and three from the Gregorian. These prayers are followed by psalmody (unspecified) and five *capitula*, including three which appear at this point in the manuscript of the 'Gelasian of the eighth century' written by Godelgaudus of Rheims. Amongst them we find the earliest instance of the antiphon *Requiem aeternam*. Edmund Bishop suggests that the antiphon may have been in use as a private devotion in England in the eighth century, as canon 27 of the council of Cloveshoe (747) speaks of praying for the dead in the following terms: *Domine, secundum magnam misericordiam tuam da requiem animae illius, atque ei, pro tua immensa pietate, gaudia lucis aeternae donare cum tuis sanctis dignare*.[12] This would certainly be congruous with Alcuin's use of it, as he drew so heavily on Spanish prayers current in England and Ireland for much of the material in his Supplement. The two prayers, *Deus vitae dator* and *Deus qui humanarum animarum*, which Alcuin provides to be said after the washing of the body, and the two prayers immediately before the burial, *Obsecramus misericordiam tuam* and *Deus apud quem mortuorum*, are all taken from Mozarabic sources. Three of the five prayers after burial are from the Gelasian, but only one of these, *Debitum humani corporis*, is prescribed at this point in the Gelasian rite, the other two, *Oremus fratres carissimi pro anima* and *Deus qui iustis supplicationibus*, are from the Gelasian prayers preceding burial and immediately after death has occurred, respectively. The two remaining post-burial prayers, *Temeritatis quidem est* and *Tibi Domine commendamus*, are from the Mozarabic. The occurrence of the latter as the final prayer in Rheinau 30 provides the earliest evidence of the existence and circulation of Alcuin's Supplement at the very end of the eighth century.[13] These prayers from Alcuin's Supplement exerted a wide influence, and most of them are found, though not necessarily in Alcuin's precise order, in later medieval rites.

The character of these early rites, as Philippeau accurately observes, is the clear incorporation of the necessary stages of burial into a liturgical pattern. Later developments, however, led away from this, an important influence being the growth of special monastic liturgies of burial, where meditation on death and a lengthier and more complex ceremonial gradually intruded upon the original simple structure.[14]

Typical of the ordering of death and burial within monastic communities is the practice of the Cluniacs.[15]

The monk who feels the moment of his death approaching is bidden to summon the abbot or prior in order that he may confess his sins and receive the sacrament of unction. He is then brought into the presence of the assembled chapter, supported by two of the brethren, and publicly confesses his omissions in his duties towards God and his neighbour. The prior then absolves him, and the community respond 'Amen'. The sick man is then taken back to his bed, where he lies to receive Holy Unction. The sacrament is administered by the priest of the week, who comes in procession to the infirmary with servers, holy water, cross, and candles, and with the rest of the community following in attendance. Unction is given whilst psalms are recited, and the sick man then receives communion, after which the community withdraws, leaving the staff of the infirmary to watch over the sick man, lest he die unnoticed. A cross and lighted candles are placed at the head of the bed. When the moment of death approaches, the sick man is laid on a hair-shirt and is sprinkled with ashes, and the cloister door is beaten rapidly to summon the community. All brethren outside of choir must leave whatever they are doing immediately and go to the infirmary. When they are assembled, the creed is said and (should the moment of death be delayed) litanies, with the responses *Ora pro eo*, and psalmody. At the moment of death the prior commends the departing soul to God with the prayers *Pie recordationis affectu, Deus cui omnia vivunt*, and *Suscipe, Domine, animam servi tui*. The community then go to the Lady Chapel of the monastery to sing vespers of the dead followed by mattins, at the end of which the collect *Omnipotens sempiterne Deus* is said. A little after this bells are rung, and a second cross, holy water, lights, and incense are brought, and the body is washed and placed on the bier by those of equal standing in the community. The body is clothed in a shirt and a habit with hood, and the hands are joined across the breast. The bier is then carried into the church, where from that time there is continuous recitation of psalmody until burial, only interrupted by the offices and mass. The night is divided into three watches, assigned to the two sides of the choir and the children with their masters respectively. Mass the next morning is offered for the dead, and the deacon is directed to cense the body after the censing of the altar. When mass is ended, the body is carried to a place of burial whilst the community in procession chant psalms. On arrival at the grave, it is censed by the priest and sprinkled with holy water, after which it is laid in the grave and earth is cast upon it. The procession returns after the burial to the tolling of bells.

A number of these monastic ceremonies connected with burial and some further ones are discussed by Durandus of Mende (1230–1296) in his *Rationale divinorum officiorum*. He refers, for instance, to the custom of placing the dying man on a bed of ashes, because the body 'is ashes, and it will return to ashes'.[16] Durandus cites the example of St Martin as his authority for this, but the custom is commonly reported, as in the life of Aelred of Rievaulx, who was placed, when death approached, *super cilicium et cinerem more monachorum, filiorumque turba circa illum adunata*.[17] In the *Rationale* Durandus also mentions the reading of the Passion by the bedside of the dying man, but suggests that this should only be done if the dying man is literate. When death has occurred, the bells should be rung—a custom reaching back at least to the seventh century, as Bede tells of a nun in a distant convent hearing the death of the abbess Hilda in this way.[18] It is also referred to in later monastic regulations, such as the eleventh century constitutions of Lanfranc, which require the tolling of the bell at the moment of death so that those hearing it may pray for the departed by saying the *Subvenite*.[19] In describing the funeral procession from the church to the grave, Durandus states that the bier should be born by those of equal rank to the deceased, though women are to be excluded from this. Three halts are to be made on the way. The grave itself is to be sprinkled with holy water and censed, in order that the stench of the body may be removed, and laurel may be placed in the grave to signify the continuing life of those dying in Christ. The body, Durandus states, should be placed in the grave with the head to the west and the feet to the east, in a posture of prayer, but as though ready to leap up at the Last Day.[20] We find the same tradition of burial in other writers, for instance, Hildebert of Lavardin, archbishop of Tours (1056–1133): 'When we bury the dead, we bury them in this manner, that the feet may be towards the east and the head towards the west.'[21] Moreover, Durandus notes, Christians should be buried in the clothes of their rank, and those in holy orders with the *instrumenta* of their order. All, Durandus believes, ought to be buried with boots or shoes on their feet so that they may be prepared at the appearance of the Judge! This leads him to a discussion of whether men will be naked or clothed at the Last Day—an argument he concludes in favour of clothing from the Gospel narratives of the Transfiguration and the Easter appearances.[22]

It was in a monastic context that the office of the dead was developed. In its established form it consisted essentially of two parts, Vespers of the dead, commonly known as the *Placebo*, from the words of the opening antiphon *Placebo Domino in regione vivorum*, and Matins and Lauds, known popularly as 'the Dirge', from the opening antiphon, *Dirige*. In the Sarum rite, to take an English example, the *Placebo* was said in the room where death occurred whilst the body was prepared for burial. It consisted of five psalms with appropriate antiphons, the Magnificat, Kyries and Lord's Prayer, and two collects. Psalm cxlvi, *Lauda, anima mea*, was said and not sung after the Magnificat—a curious treatment for the one psalm in the office which has an exultant character.[23] Matins and Lauds, which were sung the following day, were usually treated as a continuous office. Matins consists of a series of three nocturns, each built around a lesson from Job. This is a tradition which is already found in *Ordo* XLIX, with its provision that, when the body is brought into the church they chant psalms or responses, followed by the mass or readings from Job until the time of burial. Each nocturn commences with three psalms together with antiphons followed by responses and the Lord's prayer, after which the lessons are read with responses after each of them. Lauds has a similar structure to Vespers: five psalms with antiphons; the *Benedictus* with 'I am the Resurrection and the Life' as the antiphon; the Kyries; Lord's Prayer; Psalm cxliv, *Benedictus Dominus;* responses and prayers.

Durandus interprets the office, and indeed all the rites for the dead, in a way which emphasizes the penal nature of death, and this serves as a reminder of the change of emphasis which occurred in the liturgy of death and burial in the Western Church during the Middle Ages. The pattern of the office of the dead, he points out, is similar to the liturgy for the last three days of Holy Week, the *triduum sacrum*, when the *Gloria*, Alleluias, blessings before lessons, and other joyful responses are omitted. In the office of the dead, he asserts, there should not be rejoicing but rather sorrow and mourning, and all canticles of exultation and joy should be omitted.[24]

This sombre note is particularly apparent in the sequence, *Dies irae*. This did not become the official sequence of the mass for the dead until the reform of the Roman liturgy in 1570, though it was used as such in other places earlier. Its original liturgical use was as a sequence for the first Sunday in Advent.[25] Its authorship was traditionally ascribed to the Franciscan, Thomas of Celano (*c.* 1190–1260), on the strength of a remark of Bartholomew of Pisa, who names him as the author of both the life of St Francis and the *Dies irae*.[26] This attribution is now generally believed to be false, though it is true that the sequence first appears in Franciscan missals in the first half of the fourteenth century. Originally it was a *pia meditatio* on the theme of death and judgment influenced by many of the responses of the burial rites, especially the *Libera me* ('Deliver me, O Lord, from eternal death in that great day when the heavens and the earth are moved, that day, that day of wrath, ruin, and misery, that great and bitterest of days!')[27] In order to fit the sequence for liturgical use two further verses were added:

> lacrimosa dies illa,
> qua resurget ex favilla
> iudicandus homo reus;
> huic ergo parce, Deus.

pie Iesu, Domine,
dona eis requiem.

One of the marks of medieval piety in general was its special concern for the welfare of the departed. The development of this can be traced in the burial rites and offices for the dead with the increase of prayer for delivery from the pains of hell, at the expense, very often, of more primitive elements, with their paschal emphasis and prayer for entry into a place of refreshment, light, and peace. This changing mood was not, however, something confined to the burial offices, properly so called; it extended to the church's everyday worship in the multiplication of masses for the dead, the practice of obituary lists, and the wide observance of the Commemoration of All Souls. As these elements of medieval piety are important as forming part of the background to the Reformers' treatment of the medieval burial rites, it is appropriate to give them some consideration.[28]

The origins of the practices mentioned are usually considered to lie in the diptychs: lists of living and departed Christians read out in the course of the eucharist in both east and west. In the earliest surviving diptych (408) we find four categories commemorated: emperors, bishops, martyrs, and confessors. Of these, the bishops were later transferred to episcopal lists and the martyrs to martyrologies. The title of a martyrology from Carthage, thought to date from the time of the Vandal invasions, describes it as containing 'the birthdays of the martyrs and the obit days of the bishops whose anniversaries are celebrated by the Church of Carthage'. Strictly speaking, this is a mixture of martyrology and diptych, but the practice grew of including the departed by special mention at the end of the list. By the ninth century we find diptychs headed 'Names of departed kings' and 'Names of departed bishops' at Fulda. Practice was, however, far from uniform, and Thurston cites examples of different titles such as *necrologium*, *liber vitae*, and *martyrologium*.[29] The practice of reading the names publicly became impracticable as the lists extended, and expedients were devised whereby the commemoration of the departed in the prayer *Hanc igitur* at the Mass was modified by such clauses as 'Whose names are seen written below in this brief (*breviario*)'.[30] Founders and benefactors of monastic houses made gifts on condition that their names were remembered, and this practice was extended in the form of compacts with associated monastic houses and with particular individuals. Molinier cites Bede's request to Edfrid, bishop of Lindisfarne, that he would pray for his soul, and his acceptance of Edfrid's promise to write his name in the album of his congregation.[31] The agreement mutually to commemorate their departed made between the communities of St Gall and Reichenau may serve as an example of a compact between two monastic houses. When the news of the death of a brother in one community was received in the other, the priest-monks were to celebrate three masses for the departed that same day, and lay religious were to recite the psalter and sing the vigils. Seven days later, thirty psalms were recited with intention for the departed and on the thirtieth day each priest said a mass and the monks read fifty psalms. At the beginning of each month there was a reciprocal celebration of a general office for the dead, the names of the last of the brethren to die being publicly recited. On 14 November there was an annual solemn celebration, when each priest celebrated three masses, the whole psalter was recited, and vigils were sung.[32]

There was an inevitable tendency to complexity inherent in this pattern as time passed and the number of commemorations increased. It is not surprising, therefore, that towards the end of the Middle Ages the stipulations laid down in these agreements, whether they were between monastic houses or between communities and inviduals, became less and less demanding. There was a corresponding growth in the custom of laymen being clothed as monks on their deathbeds in order that they might secure the greater benefits entailed in the more elaborate arrangements made between religious houses. It is thought that the phrase *frater ad succurrendum* refers to those who died, having made the necessary arrangements, before the actual clothing ceremony could be performed.[33] The tendency to exact heavy payments for the privilege of being entered on the obituary rolls also grew, as did the development of various categories of commemoration, for example the *Maius*, *Mediocre*, *Minus* and *Parvum* used at Jumièges.[34] From the twelfth century the commemoration often contained solemn absolutions, and in the fifteenth century we hear of the chapter at Bourges going in procession on the first ten days of each month to the tombs of seven benefactors buried in the cathedral to give the absolutions.[35] The increase in the services demanded became overwhelming in many places, and we find many instances of obituaries being combined together and even being totally neglected. As an example of the commemorations which could be demanded, we can point to the situation of the monks of Jumièges in the fifteenth century, who had 225 anniversaries of all kinds to keep and about 260 ferial days in which to do so.[36]

The development of All Souls' Day was a logical extension of the custom of keeping anniversaries. We have already noted how in the ninth century the monasteries of St Gall and Reichenau kept an annual solemn commemoration on 14 November for their departed brethren, but it was not until the eleventh century that 2 November became universally observed. The selection of the day was a consequence of the decree of St Odilo of Cluny in 998 addressed to the Cluniac monasteries, requesting that, 'as the feast of all the blessed saints was already celebrated throughout the Church of God, so it seemed desirable that at Cluny they should also keep with joyous affection the memory of all the faithful departed, who have lived from the beginning of the world until the end'.[37] It is possible, as Thurston suggests, that the selection of 2 November may have grown out of the custom of reciting the psalter, or at least part of it, for the departed at the beginning of each month with the result that the conjunction of this with All Saints' Day led to a special commemoration at this time.[38] The original Cluniac custom spread rapidly, and by the early thirteenth century All Souls' Day was widely observed.[39]

Monastic influences elaborated the liturgy of burial and at Rome, always conservative and slow to change in liturgical matters, the changes followed on the appearance of Romano-Germanic liturgical books there in the tenth century. Later Roman developments were much influenced by the liturgical work of the Franciscans, and the ritual of the last Sacraments, adapted and abbreviated from the Pontifical of Innocent III, which appears in the Franciscan *Regula* breviary of the thirteenth century, is considered by some to be the immediate forerunner of the revised Roman Ritual of 1614.[40] The changes were in several directions. The inclusion of prayers asking God to absolve sinners from their offences brought the note of judgment to the fore. Distinct rites were produced for the burial of clergy of different ranks, and there was a gradual loss of liturgical interest in the actual care and preparation of the body for burial, together with a shifting of emphasis to prayer in the presence of the body and the funeral mass. The beginning of this development can perhaps be seen in the omission of the Gelasian prayers for the washing of the body in the 'Pontifical of Prudentius of Troyes' (in reality a Benedictine missal of the twelfth century). In this, after the commendation of the soul immediately death has occurred, the order moves straight to the prayers to be said after the washing of the body.[41] Another example of this same omission of liturgical provision for the washing of the body is to be found in the *Manuale Norvegicum*, where the prayers assigned to this part of the rite in the thirteenth-century manuscript are omitted in the fifteenth-century one.[42]

The more elaborate monastic rites and special services for the burial of the clergy led to some simpler forms being evolved for 'non-solemn' funerals for the laity in large towns. Gy cites a fifteenth-century example of this: the parish ritual of St André-des-Arcs in Paris, with its simple provision of *Libera*, de *Profundis*, and a prayer of absolution.[43] The final reform of the Roman funeral ritual after Trent—the last of the liturgical reforms to be carried through—was in large measure a product of this process. This burial liturgy, contained in the Ritual promulgated by Paul V in 1614 was, in fact, the first official Roman Ritual, but the way for it had been prepared by the *Liber sacerdotalis* of Alberto Castellani (1523) and the Ritual of Cardinal Santori (†1602). The latter in particular served as a basis for the 1614 ritual.

Since this ritual was that used until very recently in the Roman Church, and since it may in some ways be seen as the final stage of medieval developments, it is appropriate to summarise its provisions before turning to a consideration of the Reformers' treatment of the medieval rites.

The ritual provides for a procession from the house of the departed to the church; the office of the dead; the funeral mass followed by the absolution; and a procession to the place of burial followed by the burial proper.

On arrival at the house *De profundis* with the antiphon *Si iniquitates* is said. The funeral procession to the church is then formed, and the body is carried thither, whilst Psalm li, *Miserere*, is intoned, with the antiphon *Exultabunt Domino ossa humiliata* and concluding with *Requiem aeternam*. On arrival at the church the bier is carried inside to the responsory *Subvenite sancti Dei*, and it is placed before the altar, surrounded with candles. The office of the dead is then said, with Matins including the traditional lessons from Job. The office being ended, the Lord's Prayer and a short series of responses are said (*A porta inferi, Requiem aeternam*, &c.) followed by the prayer, *Absolve, quaesumus, Domine, animam famuli tui.* Then the funeral mass is celebrated, at the end of which the ministers proceed to the bier and say the prayer *Non intres in iudicium,* and then the responsory *Libera me Domine de morte aeterna,* the Kyries, and the Lord's Prayer; and the bier is sprinkled with holy water, the absolutions concluding with the prayer *Deus, cui proprium est misereri.* The absolutions are followed by the procession to the place of burial, which leaves the church to the recitation of the anthem *In Paradisum.* On arrival at the grave, should it not already have been blessed, the priest blesses it, saying the prayer *Deus cuius miseratione,* and the body is placed in the grave. The *Benedictus* is then said, with *Ego sum resurrectio et vita* as the antiphon, followed by the Kyries, Lord's Prayer, and responses as at the end of the office. Then, after the prayer *Fac quaesumus* has been said, the priest makes the sign of the cross over the grave saying the response *Requiem aeternam,* followed by *Requiescat in pace.* On the return from the place of burial to the church *De profundis* is again said with the antiphon, *Si iniquitates.*

This order, especially if the greater part of the office for the dead is omitted as the rubrics allow, is considerably shorter than the developed medieval pattern. It indicates, as Philippeau has rightly observed, a move away from the primitive sanctification of death and the material actions associated with it, and even from the later pattern of prayers for the dead set between the various funeral actions, to being a meditation on death on the occasion of the obsequies of a particular individual.[43] We have already observed how the note of judgment and the terror of death came to replace the earlier emphasis on entry into the joy of paradise in the course of the Middle Ages, and this sombre note is still apparent in the 1614 Ritual. It is notable in the psalmody, in which the opening psalm of the old Cologne order and *Ordo XLIX, In exitu Israel,* with its paschal and baptismal associations, has been replaced by *De Profundis,* and the tone of the psalmody in general is penitential.

The Ritual of 1614 was an attempt to make the medieval services manageable, and, as far as possible, to bring order out of chaos, for, by the end of the Middle Ages, the early pattern of the burial rites had become swamped by a mass of psalmody, antiphons, and responses, and were in their full compass only possible to use within the context of a monastic community. Only there was it possible for the demand that a body should not be left before burial without watchers beside it reciting psalms, to be in any way generally fulfilled. Yet even the monasteries were unable, and often unwilling, to cope with a system in which the rights of individuals and other communities vied for a place in the all-important prayer for the departed. The reform of 1614, inadequately as it appreciated the primitive pattern of Christian burial, was, therefore, important and necessary. But it had of course been long preceded by the work of the Reformers outside the Roman Church, who radically reconstructed, and in some cases all but abolished, the order for the burial of the dead, and it is to their work that we must now turn.

5 Reformation and Post-Reformation rites

The Reformation burial rites were all severe simplifications of the medieval pattern. Indeed, on the left wing of the Reformation there were no burial rites at all, the act of burial being viewed as simply a convenient way of disposing of a dead body without particular religous significance, and without the need of any special liturgical forms. Where such forms were provided, as amongst Lutherans and Anglicans, and (minimally) amongst Calvinists, possible references to purgatory were strictly excised, and forms of prayer for the dead were almost completely discarded. The elaborate structure of the medieval burial rites was replaced by a simpler order, and an often lengthy homily was substituted for the earlier multiplicity of psalms and antiphons.

The Lutheran Orders

It was the Lutheran revisions which were the most conservative in comparison with the medieval rites, in keeping with Luther's acceptance of much traditional Christian practice as *adiaphora*, things indifferent. One of the earliest and most interesting examples of Lutheran reform of the burial liturgy is found, not as an actual burial order, but as part of the proposals for the reformation of the church in Hesse put forward by the Synod of Homberg in October 1526. Francis Lambert (1487–1530), a former Franciscan from Avignon, who had been a convert of Zwingli's and a pupil of Luther's, was instrumental in the drawing up of these proposals. The section which deals with funerals proposes that psalms may be read at the discretion of the bishop, and that prayer should be offered for the living, 'that they may live and die in holiness'. All should be in the vernacular, unless all those present understand Latin. Extravagant funeral ceremonies should be avoided out of respect for the poor. A homily in which the word of God is sincerely preached is commended, but there should be no mention of purgatory, 'for it is only by faith that God purges and cleanses his church from sin'.[1] These particular proposals were never put into effect, being superseded by the Saxon ordinances, but they are good examples of the Reformers' attitude towards funeral practice. The plea for the restraint of funeral expenses and the condemnation of unnecessary pomp is one which regularly recurs in the literature concerning burial, and it is no surprise to discover that the Reformers aimed at simplicity in this matter. The emphasis on 'a sincere preaching of the Word of God', prayers in the common tongue, and the avoidance of purgatorial doctrine are common Reformation emphases and need no comment.

There are a number of local variants of the early Lutheran orders, but in general they follow a similar pattern.[2] The Brandenburg-Nürnberg Church Order of 1533, like that of Calenburg, has no provision for a service in church at all, but begins at the grave-side with the *Benedictus* (which occurs as one of the canticles said on the way to the grave in some of the medieval rites), or with Psalm xc, *Domine, refugium*. This is followed by the hymn *Media vita*, or the antiphon *Ego sum resurrectio*, or a German hymn, such as Luther's translation of the *Media vita, Mitten unsers lebens zeyt wir mit dem todt umfangen*. The burial then takes place, apparently in silence, and the service concludes with a sermon, delivered either at the grave-side or back at the house of the deceased. The Calenberg order has no introductory psalm or canticle, and begins with the *Media vita* and *De Profundis* in German, followed by the burial proper, a sermon, a lesson (John xi.16–44), and an invitation to alms. The Brandenburg Church Order (1540) and the proposals of Hermann of Wied, archbishop of Cologne, in his *Einfaltigs Bedencken einer christlichen Reformation* (1543), are more detailed. The latter was translated into English as *A simple and religious consultation* in 1547, and had a general influence on the shape of the English Prayer Book.

The Brandenburg order begins with the funeral procession, preceded by a cross, going to the grave, with those present reciting the *Media vita* and *De profundis* in German, concluding with the response, *Libera me*, and burial then follows. After this provision is made for a short service in church. This begins with a German version of the *Nunc dimittis*, followed by lessons from Job

75

and St Paul (I Corinthians xv) on the theme of resurrection, with responses or German hymns being sung between the readings. The *Benedictus* with the antiphon *Ego sum resurrectio* is then sung, followed by a German collect asking that, as God has delivered men from sin and death by the death of Christ, so through his resurrection they may enter into eternal life. A response, *Si bono credimus*, and an offertory sentence, *Si enim credimus*, lead to the epistle (I Thessalonians iv.12–17) and gospel (John xi.21–27), and the rite concludes with the repetition of the response, *Si bono credimus*.

The Cologne order drawn up by Hermann is not quite so elaborate. The section of the English version headed 'Of Buriynge' begins with a warning that those dying manifestly outside the faith of Christ are not to be buried with the faithful, and then proceeds to set out the pattern of the funeral procession and burial.

> While the corpes is caried furth, it shal be laweful to synge in the mydde waye (i.e. *Media vita*) the psalme From the deepe, or suche other lyke songes.
>
> And that the people maye be more diligently admonished of those thynges, which are to be considered aboute burials, it shall not be unprofitable, if a certeyne tyme of buriall shall be appoynted, at whiche tyme some apte place of scripture maye be reade with a short exposition of the place, and admonition, and exhortation derived out of the same, wherein thynges of thys sorte shal be sette forth. Chiefely the exceading greatnes of synne, and of the wrath of God, whereupon death ensued.
>
> Secondly the singuler, and inestimable benefite of the redemption of Christ . . . And if there be anie notable proues of goddes goodnes declared towardes the deade person in his lyfe, or death, the ministre shall declare and prayse the same.[3]

I Thessalonians iv.12–17 is then proposed as the lesson to be read, with the suggestion that Luke vii.11–15 (the raising of the widow's son at Nain) and Matthew ix.18, 19, 23–26 (the raising of Jairus' daughter) be substituted at the funerals of young men and young women respectively. A sermon is then to follow, of which two examples are given. Their conclusions illustrate well the understanding of the Christian hope which the Reformers strove to inculcate in their burial offices. Hermann's first sermon ends thus:

> Seeinge then that thys our brother [was baptised, confirmed, received communion, and] finally departed in the confession of

Christ, we have good hope . . . that at the sounde of the trompe of the archangel, in a moment, in the twinkling of an eye, he shal come out of hys grave to meete Christ, and shall obteyne with al the sayntes the inheritance of the heauenly kingdome, and enioye euerlastinge blissfulnes.

Wherefore lette us also give thankes to oure Lorde God for him, and lette us besech hym ernestly that he wyll brynge us to the true knowledge of Christ through the holi gost, whereby we maye ouer-come death, and be kepte in death itselfe unto everlastinge life, through Christe our Lorde . . .[4]

After the sermon the Lord's Prayer is said, then *Dominus vobiscum* followed by two collects. The English version of these runs as follows:

Almightie God, and moste louynge father, encrease in us the belefe of the resurrection, whereunto thou haste called us thorowe oure Lorde Jesus Christe, that beinge grounded upon thys beliefe, we maye comforte oure selves in the death of thys oure brother (or sister) whose bodie we have now committed to the earth, accordyng to thy ordinaunce, and that we maye also comforte oure selves in other calamities, whyche in thys valleye of teares, we worthyly suffre for oure synnes. Further that we maye lifte up oure myndes, and thoughtes unto the heauenly lyfe to come, and seke the thinges that are aboue, where Christe thy sonne is, sittinge at thy right hande, finally that diinge to sinne daily, we maye serue the al the dayes of oure lyfe in all sanctification, and righteousness throughe the same Christe oure Lorde.

We gyve thanckes unto the almyghtye God, heauenlie father for that thou hast vouchsafed to cal this our brother (or sister) to the knowledge of thi deare sonne, and his communion, and to preserve him in the same and nowe to sende for hym, and remoue him to thy kingdome. Graunte us we besech thee, thorough the same thy sonne, that in thys place, and in al other we maie truly acknowlege our synnes, ernestly lament them, and knowe, and prayse the dayly more and more in the newnes of lyfe, and that so beynge strengthened with good hope, we maie looke for that blessed hope and appearinge of the glorie of the greate God and oure Saviour Jesus Christe, which liveth God and raigneth with the in the unite of the holye goste through out al generations. Amen.

Finally, Herman adds, 'for the consolacion of the faythfull in the Lord and mouinge the zeal of godlines', a lesson shall be read at the grave-side. This is to be taken from I Corinthians xv, Philippians iii.20–21, or Romans vi.8–12. A lesson of this kind at the grave-side is also found in the Hanover Church order of 1536, where the pastor is directed to read from Scripture concerning death and the resurrection of Christians.[5]

In Lutheran churches outside Germany similar burial offices were used. The Norwegian rite, for instance, which was established by the Church ordinance of 1537, opens with the *Benedictus* or a psalm or other canticle, followed by *Media vita*. The body is then committed to the grave, the Creed and *Nunc dimittis* are said, and, after a short exhortation, the Lord's Prayer ends the rite.[6]

Of particular interest are the Swedish services drawn up by Olavus Petri in 1529. These include a rite for the 'Hallowing of the Dead' as well as an order for burial.[7] The 'Hallowing of the dead' replaces the old medieval prayers to be said after death, whilst the body is laid out and prepared for burial. It begins with a rubric which states: 'If occasion be that the corpse is to be hallowed before it is borne from the house, it may be done on this fashion or such other as may befit a Christian. The priest may first make an exhortation, and comfort the friends of the departed, that they do not sorrow and trouble themselves overmuch for his sake.'

The exhortation Olavus provides reminds those present of the Christian hope, and emphasizes that death 'is called in the scriptures a sleep, so that Christian men who die are said to sleep in the Lord until the last resurrection on the day of judgement.' This reflects Luther's understanding of the sleep of the soul between death and the Last Day.[8] There follows a lesson, John xi.21–27, which Olavus probably took from the Office of the Dead in the *Manuale Lincopense*, and a further exhortation to Christian hope.

> The heathen, that have no knowledge of the resurrection from the dead, are greatly troubled and grieved that they lose their friends, for they have not the hope that they will some time receive them again. But we Christians, who know that we shall receive them in better estate than when we lose them, have no such trouble; but rather do we meditate upon it, so that we too are in readiness, when God shall call us from this poor and wretched world, as he hath done with our friend.

There is then a final prayer, including a carefully worded petition for the departed.

> . . . Turn now thy fatherly countenance toward us thy poor children, and hear our prayer, that if this our departed brother (sister) whom thou through death hast called from this miserable life, be in such an

estate that our prayers can avail for his (her) good, thou wilt be gentle and merciful to him (her), O heavenly Father, preserve him (her) in Abraham's bosom, and at the last judgement raise him (her) up in the resurrection of the just.

The burial office itself is very simple. The body is placed immediately in the grave, and the priest casts earth three times upon it with the words, 'From earth art thou come, and earth thou shalt become again. Jesus Christ thy Saviour shall raise thee up again at the last day.' There follows a prayer for God's mercy on the bereaved, and their own preparation for death, together with a petition framed in the same cautious way as in the prayer in the Hallowing of the Dead, that 'if the estate of the departed permits, God will grant him rest 'with thy chosen friends, Abraham, Isaac, and Jacob'. Whilst the grave is filled in, hymns may be sung, and Olavus provides two, the first a paraphrase of the *Media vita*, the second of Psalm li. There follows a lesson (I Thessalonians iv.13–18)[9] and a final exhortation, again stressing the Christian hope of resurrection.

One of the notable features of the Lutheran burial services is the regular occurrence of the sequence *Media vita*, and it was from its use in Lutheran burial offices in Germany that it was included in the burial office of the English Prayer Book. The sequence has a curious history. It is first found in an eleventh-century manuscript, and occurs also in the twelfth-century Mozarabic Breviary. Traditionally, but without any real evidence, ascribed to Notker, the ninth-century monk of St Gall, who was the author of many sequences, it is said to have been used at Compline on the eve of the Fourth Sunday in Lent, and it appears in the Sarum Breviary as the antiphon to the *Nunc dimittis* from the Third to the Fifth Sunday in Lent. In medieval Germany it acquired the character of a war-song, and appears to have been used as a kind of incantation to be chanted as men rode into battle. The practice was condemned by canon xxi of the council of Cologne in 1310 which forbade both the cursing of others and the singing of the *Media vita* against them.[10] By the fifteenth century it had been turned into a German hymn, and it was on the basis of this that Luther composed his *Mitten wir im leben sind*. The version translated in the English Prayer Book differs in its ending from that found in the Sarum Breviary. Dowden argues from this that Cranmer based his text on the English version of Luther's hymn found in Miles Coverdale's *Goostly Psalmes and Spirituall Songes*. This appeared in England some time before 1539, together with Coverdale's own translation from the original Latin. The first verse of Coverdale's hymn reads as follows:

In the myddest of our lyvynge
Death compaseth us rounde about:
Who sholde us now sucour brynge
By whose grace we maye come out?
Even thou, Lorde Jesu, alone:
It doth oure hartes sore greve truly
That we have offended the.
O Lord God most holy
O Lord God most holy
O Lord God most myghtie
O holy and mercyfull Savioure,
Thou most worthy God eternall,
Suffre us not at our last hour
For any death from the to fall.
Kirieleyson.[11]

The latter part is echoed in the words of the Prayer Book version: 'But spare us, Lord most holy, O God moste mighty, o holy and mercifull sauiour, thou moste worthy iudge suffre us not at our last houre for any paines of death to fal from the.'

The Lutheran burial offices were, as we have seen, simple orders, strongly biblical in their phraseology, but making use of a certain amount of traditional material. The sermon as an obligatory part of the order is an innovation and many of the most ancient prayers have disappeared, with their reference to a place of refreshment, light, and peace, and their petitions that the departed may be brought to enjoy the fellowship of the Old Testament patriarchs and the saints. The prayers are much more concerned with admonishing and exhorting the living than with commendation of the dead, and there is a striking emphasis on the hope of resurrection at the Last Day, in contrast to the immediate expectation of the joy of paradise or deliverance from purgatorial fires. Despite the conscious scripturalism of the Lutheran rites, there is little trace of the paschal imagery of the early funeral liturgy, but this is perhaps not surprising in the light of the medieval development of the themes of death, judgment, and eternal punishment, and the dark sentiments of the fifteenth century expressed in such things as the manuals of preparation for death known as the *Ars moriendi*, and the representations of the Dance of Death.

In the Reformed tradition it is often a question of discussing the absence of any burial rite rather than the nature of the rite itself. Although the practice of burial could scarcely be dismissed as unbiblical, and quite obviously there had to be some way of disposing of the dead, the holding of special services at the time of burial was more difficult to justify. Calvin himself defended them on the grounds that burial itself was a powerful witness against pagan denials of the resurrection, and wrote forcibly to this effect in the *Institutes*.

> But in order that this gross ignorance might not excuse anyone, by an unbelievable prompting of nature men always had before their eyes an image of the resurrection. Why the sacred and inviolable custom of burial, but as an earnest of the new life? And no one can claim that this arose out of error, for burial rites were always kept up among the holy patriarchs; and God willed that the same custom remain among the Gentiles so that an image of the resurrection set before them might shake off their drowsiness. Now although that ceremony was unprofitable, it is useful to us if we wisely look to its purpose. For it is a weighty refutation of unbelief that all together professed what no one believed.[12]

A little further on he re-emphasises this argument.

> For why should a burial rite arise . . . unless to let men know that a new life was prepared for the bodies laid away?
>
> Spices and other symbols of immortality also looked to the very same end as sacrifices to mitigate the obscurity of teaching under the law. It was not superstition that gave rise to this practice, since we see the Spirit no less attentive to the burial rites about to be narrated than the chief mysteries of the faith. And Christ commends this as no mean office (Matthew xxvi.10), surely for no other reason than that it raises our eyes from gazing upon a grave that corrupts and effaces everything, to the vision of renewal. Besides the very careful observance of this ceremony, which is approved in the patriarchs, is proof enough that it was to them a rare and precious aid to faith.[13]

It is clear, however, that it was primarily the act of burial itself, and the care taken to see that it was performed, which was of significance to Calvin, and when it came to drawing up regulations for burial in the new ecclesiastical constitution for Geneva in 1541 he wrote as follows.

> Qu'on ensepuelisse honestement les mortz au lieu ordonné. De la suyte et compaignye, nous la laissons à le discretion d'n chascun.

Il sera bon que les porteurs ayent serment à nous d'empescher touttes superstitions contraires à la parole de Dieu, de n'en point porter à l'heure indeue, et faire rapporte si quelqu'un estoit mort subitement, affin d'obrier à touz inconveniens qui en pourroient advenir.

Item après leur mort de ne les porter plustot de douze heures et non plus tard que vingt et quatre.[14]

What the Reformed understanding of burial amounted to in practice is clearly shown in John Knox's Genevan Service Book of 1556. This simply states that 'the corps is reuerently brought to the graue, accompagnied with the congregation withe owte any further ceremonies, which beyng buriede the minister goethe to the church, if it be not farre off, and maketh some comfortable exhortation to the people, touching deathe and resurrection'.[15] This same provision appears in the Scottish Book of Common Order of 1564, with the exception that the words concerning the minister are expanded by the phrase 'if he be present and required'. The *Book of Discipline* (1560) gives further details, stating that it is 'most expedient that the dead be conveyed to the place of burial with some honest company of the church, without either singing or reading, yea without all kind of ceremony heretofore used, other than that the dead be committed to the grave with such gravity and sobriety as those that be present may seem to fear the judgments of God, and to hate sin which is the cause of death.' 'Yet notwithstanding', Knox adds, 'we are not so precise but that we are content that particular kirks may use them in that behalf as they will answer to God and the Assembly of the Universal Kirk, gathered within the realm.'[16] A further paragraph forbids funeral sermons on the grounds that, if people despise instruction in ordinary discourses, they are unlikely to benefit from sermons on special occasions. To allow funeral sermons was, moreover, to open the way to class-distinctions in funerals. Nevertheless, the General Assembly of 1562 appointed an order of services, including the Burial of the Dead, which was to be 'according to the use of the Kirk of Geneva', and we know that funeral sermons were in use there during Knox's ministry. In fact, sermons seem to have continued at funerals in some parts of Scotland at least until 1638, when the General Assembly passed an act forbidding funeral services. Before that time, the common attitude seems to have been that expressed by Cowper in his draft order of 1629, where we read, in the section headed 'The Maner of Buriall', that:

the exequies used in some reformed churches, and performed with solemn reading of some parts of Scripture, prayers and singing we do not dislike; as serving to stir up the minds of men into a careful consideration of the estate both here and hereafter. But our church not being accustomed therewith, doth leave it to the discretion of the Minister, who being present at the Burial, and required, ought not to refuse to make some comfortable exhortation to the people touching death and resurrection to life.[17]

The *Directory* of 1644, which was in fact a translation of a book of discipline compiled by the English Puritan divine, Walter Travers, in about 1586, again reproduces quite clearly the Calvinist conviction that burials ought to be performed decently and reverently, but that there was little more to be said. The section headed 'Concerning Burial of the Dead' reads as follows:

When any person departeth this life, let the dead body, upon the day of burial, be decently attended from the house to the place appointed for public burial, and there immediately interred, without any ceremony.

And because the custom of kneeling down, and praying by or towards the dead corpse, and other such usages, in the place where it lies, before it be carried to burial, are superstitious; and for that praying, reading, and singing, both in going to and at the grave, have been grossly abused, are no way beneficial to the dead, and have proved many ways hurtful to the living; therefore, let all such things be laid aside.

Howbeit we judge it very convenient, that the Christian friends which accompany the dead body to the place appointed for public burial, do apply themselves to meditations and conferences suitable to the occasion: and that the minister, as upon other occasions, so at this time, if he be present, may put them in remembrance of their duty.

That this shall not extend to deny any civic respects or differences at the burial, suitable to the rank and condition of the party deceased whilst he was living.[18]

As this last paragraph indicates, the relegation of burial to little more than a secular disposal of the dead body, meant that any pomp and parade at funerals was entirely secular, as was indeed the case with the funerals of the Scottish nobility. The reference to praying by the body shows how tenaciously the pre-Reformation vigil of the dead survived, as can also be seen in the Scottish word 'Dregy', derived from *Dirige*, used to refer to the watch kept by the corpse before burial.[19]

The treatment of burial as a civil rather than a religious act is found in an extreme form amongst the English separatist groups. Henry Barrow, for instance, the leader of just such a group which flourished between 1587 and 1593, found no authority 'in the booke of God, that it belonged to the ministers office to burie the dead'. 'It was a pollution to the Leviticall priesthood to touch a carcase or anything about it.' He objected to mourning gowns; exorbitant funeral costs; *encomia* on the dead ('to make him by his rhetorick a better Christian in his grave than he was ever in his life, or else he yerneth his money ill'); sumptuous funeral feasts; elaborate tombs; and the hanging of churches with black on the day of the funeral.[20] The funeral of the separatist Eaton is a practical illustration of this separatist attitude. His followers are said to have marched behind his body to the graveside, and without prayers, commendations, or sermon, to have thrust it into the grave and stamped earth upon it.

The Anglican services, 1549–1662

When we turn to a consideration of the burial office of the Book of Common Prayer we find a much more conservative practice than that current in the Reformed tradition. The Prayer Book of 1549 provides a service which still retains a celebration of the Eucharist as one of its elements, and which makes use of much of the traditional material in a fourfold scheme: a procession to the church or grave; the burial proper; a brief office of the dead; and a funeral eucharist. The burial could apparently either precede or follow the office for the dead (and the eucharist, if it was celebrated), for the initial rubric states that after the body has been met at 'the Churche style', the funeral procession shall 'goe either into the Churche, or towardes the graue'. The distinction was made, it has been suggested, from the necessity of burying those who died of infectious diseases immediately, with the minimum of risk to others.[21]

Three sentences are provided at the beginning of the order, of which the first two (John xi.25 and Job xix.25) are from the old offices of the dead, being an Antiphon and a Respond from Matins and Lauds respectively. The third sentence, a combination of I Timothy vi.7 and Job i.21, is original. The second section, the burial proper, begins at the grave-side with the sentence 'Man that is born of woman' (Job xiv.1), from the Sarum *Dirige*, followed by the anthem *Media vita*, which, as we have already seen, Cranmer probably took from Hermann's *Simple and Religious Consultation* and Coverdale's *Goostly Psalmes*. The priest is then directed to cast earth on the body—there is no rubric about this being done in the form of a cross—saying 'I commende thy soule to God the father almighty, and thy body to the grounde, earth to earth, asshes to asshes, dust to dust' in the hope of resurrection through Christ, which is expressed in the words of Philippians iii.21. This is followed by the anthem *Audivi vocem* ('I heard a voice from heaven', Revelation xiv.13), which was found as the anthem to the Magnificat in the Sarum Vigils of the dead. This antiphon is very anciently associated with the burial office, being prescribed in MS Rheinau 30 as the antiphon to Psalm cxvi, and in the Cologne MS 123 as the antiphon to Psalm cxliii. Two prayers follow: the first, 'We commende into thy handes of mercy', asks God to receive the soul of the departed and to give the living grace, that 'both this our brother, and we, may be found acceptable in thy sight'; the second, 'Almightie God, we geue thee hertie thankes', gives thanks for the departed, expressing the hope that he has been brought 'into sure consolacion and reste', and praying that all may attain salvation.

The third part of the burial rite is a short office of the dead, which is preceded by a rubric stating that 'these psalmes with other suffrages folowying are to be sayed in the churche either before or after the buriall of the corps'. There are three psalms, cxvi, *Dilexi quoniam*, cxlvi, *Lauda, anima mea*, and cxxxix, *Domine, probasti*, derived from Vespers of the dead and the *Commendatio animae* in the Sarum order. The first psalm (cxvi) is one of the most ancient associated with the liturgy of burial, appearing in the early eighth-century rites. The lesson, I Corinthians xv.20–58, follows, together with the Kyries, Lord's Prayer, and the suffrages familiar from the medieval rites: *Non intres in iudicium; A porta inferi; Erue domine animas eorum; Credo videre bona Domini*. Part of the prescribed lesson appears as one of the four alternative lessons in Hermann's *Consultation*. This section of the burial rite then concludes with a prayer, 'O Lorde, with whome dooe lyue the spirites of them that be dead', which is based on phrases from a number of prayers in the Sarum rite—mostly versions of the old Gelasian burial prayers, *Deus, apud quem omnia morientia vivunt*, and *Te, Domine, sancte, Pater omnipotens, aeterne Deus*, but concluding with a petition from the collect from the Sarum Mass of the Five Wounds, *Te humiliter deprecamur: ut in die iudicii ad dexteram tuam statuti*, that the departed may be set 'on the ryght hande of thy sonne Iesus Christ, among thy holy and elect, that then he maye heare with them these most swete and comfortable wordes: come to me ye blessed of my father, possesse the kyngdome whyche hath bene prepared for you from the begynning of the worlde'. The prayer includes the traditional petition that the departed 'may euer dwel in the region of lighte, with Abraham, Isaac, and Jacob, in the place where is no wepyng, sorowe, nor heauinesse'.[22] Thus the 1549 rite includes a prayer for the departed, clearly expressed in more or less traditional terms.

The final section of the 1549 service provides for the celebration of the eucharist. The introit psalm is one traditionally associated with the burial office, xlii, *Quemadmodum*. The collect 'O Mercifull god the father of oure lord Iesu Christ' is based on John xi.25, 26 and Paul's exhortation to the Thessalonians, that they should not sorrow for those who sleep in Christ; it seems to have been derived, in part at least, from a collect found at the end of the *Dirige* in bishop Hilsey's Primer of 1539.[23] Somewhat surprisingly, in the light of the prayer at the end of the burial office, this collect is not a prayer for the departed, but that the living may be raised from the death of sin to the life of righteousness, that after death they may sleep in Christ and be raised at the Last Day. The epistle provided is I Thessalonians iv.13–18, found in the Sarum rite as the epistle for the Requiem Mass when the body is present, and also found in a number of the Lutheran orders. It appears also in Hermann's *Consultation*, in which we find the following comment: 'And as concerning buriying, there is a most apte place in the first epistle of Paule, Thessalon, Chp. iiij, We wyle not that ye be ignoraunt concernying them that sleepe, etc. Out of which place there may be a sermon made.' The Gospel prescribed is John vi.37–40.

In the Prayer Book of 1552 the 1549 order was considerably truncated. Both psalmody and the funeral eucharist are abolished; the rubric directing the funeral procession to go either to the church or towards the grave is retained at the beginning, but without any subsequent indication as to which part of the rite was intended to take place in church; and the lesson is transposed to the grave-side, where it occurs in Herman's *Consultation*, and in a number of other Lutheran orders. The traditional suffrages are omitted, and only the Kyries and Lord's Prayer remain; and there are only two prayers, at the end of the service, which carefully avoid any hint of prayer for the departed. It was this last point which had been criticized by Martin Bucer and other leading Reformers in the 1549 service; Bucer wrote that 'I know that this custom of praying for the pious dead is most ancient (*pervetustam*) but, as it is our duty to prefer the divine to all human authority and since Scripture nowhere teaches us by word or example to pray for the departed . . . I wish that this commendation of the dead and prayer for them be omitted.'[24] There is no commendation of the soul in 1552, merely the committal of the body to the ground; the words of 1549, 'We commende into thy handes of mercy (most merciful father) the soule of this our brother departed, *N.*,' being replaced by the opening phrase of the second funeral sermon in Hermann's *Consultation*, 'Forasmuch as it hathe pleased almightie God of his great mercy to take unto himselfe the soule of our dere brother here departed'.[25] The prayer 'Almightie God, with whom doe lyue the spirites of them that be dead' is drastically altered. In the opening phrase 'them that departe hence in the lord' is substituted for the general expression 'them that be dead', and instead of prayer being offered that the departed may escape the gates of hell and 'paynes of eternal darckenes', and may rest in the bosom of Abraham, Isaac, and Jacob, part of the prayer, 'Almightie God, we geue thee hertie thankes', the second prayer at the burial proper in 1549, is interposed, with its reference to the departed being 'delyuered from the miseries of this wretched world'. The prayer continues with a petition that it may please God to make up the number of his elect, and concludes with the nearest that 1552 comes to prayer for the departed: 'that we wyth thys oure brother, and all other departed in the true faythe of thy holye name, maye haue our perfecte consummacion and blysse, bothe in body and soule in thy eternal and euerlastyng glory.' The final prayer, 'O Merciful God, the father of our Lorde Jesus Christ), is composed of the first part of the collect from the 1549 Funeral Eucharist, and the latter part of the prayer, 'We commend into thy handes of mercy'. The variations are interesting to compare (see p. 88). It is noteworthy that the 1552 prayer asks only that 'we' may be found acceptable in God's sight at the general resurrection and omits the petition for 'thys oure brother'.[26]

It was the 1552 burial service which was restored by Elizabeth in 1559, but various public obsequies during the two years after her succession indicated moves in a conservative direction. Bishop Griffin of Rochester died on 20 September 1558, and was buried in the style of the medieval services. We are told that his body was carried to St Magnus Martyr, where he 'had a hearse of

1549 Collect of Funeral Eucharist (latter part).	1549 'We commend . .' (latter part).	1552 Final prayer (latter part).
We mekelye beseche thee (O father) to raise vs from the death of sin vnto the life of right-eousness, that when we shal departe this lyfe, we maye slepe in him (as our hope is this our brother doeth) and at the general re-surrection in the laste daie, / both we and this oure brother de-parted, receyuing agayne our bodies, and risinge againe in thy moste gracious fauoure: maye with all thine electe Sainctes, obteine eternal ioye. Graunt this, O Lord God, by the meanes of our aduocate Iesus Christ: wiche with thee, &c. . . .	. . that when the iudg-mente shall come whiche thou haste committed to thy wel-beloued sonne, both thys oure brother, and / we, may be found acceptable in thy sight, and receyue that blessyng, whiche thy welbeloued sonne shall then pronounce to all that loue and feare thee, saying: Come ye blessed children of my father: Receyue the kyngdome prepared for you before the begyn-nyng of the worlde. Graunte thys, mercifull father, for the honour of Iesu Christe, our onely sauiour, medi-ator, and aduocate. Amen.	We mekely beseche thee (O Father) to rayse vs from the death of synne to the lyfe of righteousness, that when we shal depart this lyfe, we maye rest in him, as our hope is this our brother doth, and that at the general resurrection in the last day, / we maye be founde acceptable in thy syghte, and receyue that blessing whiche thy wel-beloued sonne shall then pronounce, to al that loue and feare thee, saying. Come ye blessed children of my father, receyue the kingdome pre-pared for you, from the beginning of the world. Graunt this we beseche thee, O mercyfull father, throughe Iesus Chryste our mediatour and redeemer. Amen.

wax and five dozen of pensils and the quire was hung with black and with his arms'. Twelve poor men in black gowns and twelve of his own servants bearing torches waited on the body, and the funeral was adorned with 'a great banner of arms and four banners of saints and eight dozen of escutcheons'. After the funeral was finished 'they all repaired to his place for dinner'.[27] On Christmas Eve the same year traditional obsequies were observed for the emperor Charles V at Westminster Abbey, where a 'rich hearse' was set up 'magnificently covered with a Pall of gold'.[28]

A year later, after the promulgation of the 1559 Prayer Book, public obsequies were held in St Paul's for Henry II of France. Parker, Grindal, Scory, and Barlow were the officiants at the services on 8 and 9 September. 'A rich Hearse' was erected in the church 'made like an Imperial Crown, sustained with eight pillars, and covered with black velvet, with a Valence fringed with gold, and richly hanged with Scutcheons, Pennons, and Banners of the French King's Arms'. The chief mourner on the first day was the marquis of Winchester, assisted by ten other peers, and heralds dressed in black. The clergy wore hoods and surplices.[29] According to Heylyn the service was the *Dirige* 'executed in the English tongue', and the order used was most likely that in the Queen's Primer of 1559, though probably not followed *au pied de la lettre*, for we are told of a proclamation by the herald at the end of the *Benedictus*, which does not appear in the *Dirige* office in the Primer. The proclamation probably replaced the traditional invitation to pray for the soul of the departed and ran as follows: 'Blessed be the King of eternal glory, who through his divine mercy hath translated the most high, puissant, and victorious prince Henry II, late the French King, from this earthly to his heavenly kingdom!'[30] The Primer *Dirige* begins with three psalms, cxvi (*Dilexi quoniam*), xli (*Beatus qui intelligit*), and clxvi (*Lauda, anima mea*), of which the first and last appear in the 1549 burial rite. There follows a series of suffrages in traditional form, praying for rest for the departed, and for delivery from the gates of hell, ending with two prayers for release from the chains and consequences of sin—a different emphasis from the prayers at this point in the 1545 Primer, which are specifically concerned with the departed. A second group of psalms, v (*Verba mea auribus*), xxvii (*Dominus illuminatio mea*), and xlii (*Quemadmodum*) is then said, followed by the anthem 'I look to see the goodness of the Lord' and a response 'Lord, grant thy people everlasting rest; and let thy everlasting light shine upon them', which is so worded as to apply to the living as well as to the dead. After the Lord's Prayer there are a series of lessons and anthems (Job x.8–13; 'I know that my redeemer liveth'; John v.24–30; I Thessalonians iv.13–15; I Corinthians xv.51–58; 'Deliver me, good Lord, from eternal death'; Psalm xxx, *Exaltabo te*; Isaiah xxxviii; Psalm lxxi, *In te Domine speravi*; 'I am the resurrection and the life'), which conclude with the Kyries and Lord's Prayer. The next response, 'Lord give thy people eternal rest', replaces 'From the gates of hel, Lord, deliver their solles', which appears at this point in the 1545 Primer, and this is followed by 'I look to see the goodness of the Lord'. There are three concluding prayers, the first, 'O God, which by the mouth of S. Paul' echoes I Thessalonians iv and the last prayer of the burial service; the second specifically petitions that God will 'be merciful to the souls of thy servants being departed from this world in the confession of thy name'; and the third replaces the 1545 petition that the prayers of the faithful may 'avail for the souls of thy servants to purge away sin and make them partakers of thy redemption', with a request that God will 'bestow the souls of thy servants . . . in the country of peace and rest, and cause them to be made partners with thy holy servants'.[31] Thus, whilst the *Dirige* of the 1559 Primer is conservative in character, there is a definite attempt to place the emphasis of such prayers for the departed as are admitted, positively on the communion of saints rather than negatively on escape from the punishments of hell.

At the obsequies for Henry II we are told that the service ended with the Magnificat and the latter part of evening prayer. The following day the Communion was celebrated, the three bishops being vested in copes and the two prebendaries in grey almuces. At the offertory the mourners offered pieces of gold for 'head-pennies'. Bishop Scory preached the funeral sermon on the subject of burial; and six of the mourners made their communion.[32]

These royal rites were clearly exceptional, but the issue of the Latin version of the Prayer Book in 1560 showed that provision had been made in this for a funeral eucharist after the pattern of the 1549 book. The letters patent made it quite clear that this was done with deliberate intent:

> We have commanded to be appended certain special things fit to be repeated at the funerals and obsequies of Christians, the aforesaid Statute of the rite of public prayer . . . promulgated in the first year of our reign, to the contrary notwithstanding.[33]

Both the collect for the Funeral Eucharist and that for the order *In commendationibus benefactorum*, which also appears in the Latin Prayer Book, permit a form of prayer for the departed in the petitions that, in the general resurrection, we will be raised together with 'this our brother' or with the departed benefactors who are commemorated.[34] The Epistle is I Thessalonians iv.13–14, and there are alternative Gospels, John vi.37–40 and John v.25–29. This provision in the Latin Prayer Book seems to have given rise to some anxiety amongst those desirous of 'reformation without tarrying for any'. The 'Articles of Government' presented to Convocation in 1563, though not accepted, ordered that no cleric 'minister or suffer to be ministered the holy communion at any burial', and when public obsequies were held for the emperor Ferdinand in 1564 Ante-communion only was said. Grindal pointed out in his sermon that 'here is no invocation or massing for the dead'.[35] There was, however, only one explicit episcopal prohibition of the funeral eucharist in Elizabeth's reign, and that was by bishop Barnes of Durham in 1577, who ordered 'that no Communion or Commemoration (as some call them) be said for the dead, or at the burials of the dead'.[36]

Other points of burial practice were also matters of contention. The bishops' *Interpretations* of 1561 permitted bells for the dying to toll only before death with 'but one short peal' after death, and two others before and after burial; and the tolling of the bell to bid prayers for the departed was forbidden.[37] In 1566 Robert Crowley, one of the signatories of the New Discipline in Frankfurt and of the Seven Articles, was cited by archbishop Parker for refusing to allow clerks vested in surplices into his church for a funeral.[38] One of the Puritan criticisms of the Prayer Book was the 'skudding' of the minister to the churchyard stile to meet the funeral cortège.[39] There were also protests from those who regarded burial as a merely secular matter, which could lead to the kind of situation such as that which arose at Coggeshall in Essex in 1607, where it was reported that one William Bird 'ys muche complayned vpon for buring the dead being a meare laye mann ... he hathe buried manye deed bodys in the parish of Coggeshall but hathe not redd the forme of buriall set forthe in the book of Common Prayer neither was ther anye minister present.'[40]

Some of the Puritan objections to the Prayer Book burial office reappeared at the Savoy Conference in 1661. The Presbyterian *Exceptions against the Book of Common Prayer* included five:

(1) that there should be a rubric stating that 'the prayers and exhortations here used are not for the benefit of the dead, but only for the instruction and comfort of the living';
(2) that the priest should be free to conduct the whole service

in church, and not to meet the cortège at the church-stile, 'for the preventing of these inconveniences which many times both ministers and people are exposed unto by standing in the open air';

(3) that the reference to the 'sure and certain hope of resurrection to eternal life' could not be said of 'persons living and dying in open and notorious sins';

(4) that the prayer 'that we with this our brother, and all other departed in the true faith of thy Holy Name, may have our perfect confirmation and bliss' could 'harden the wicked' and was 'inconsistent with the largest rational charity';

(5) that the words 'as our hope is this our brother doth' could not be used of any who had not 'by their actual repentance given any ground for the hope of their blessed estate'.[41]

The bishops replied to the second point that 'the desire that all may be said in the church, being not pretended to be for the ease of tender consciences, but of tender heads, may be helped by a cap better than a rubric'! On the other points they were of the firm opinion that, as one dare not say that any man is damned, 'it is better to be charitable, and hope the best, than rashly to condemn'.[42] In the Savoy Liturgy, drawn up by Richard Baxter, 'The Order for solemnizing the Burial of the Dead' sets out in full the Presbyterian understanding.

> It is agreeable to nature and religion, that the burial of Christians be solemnly and decently performed. As to the cases, whether the corpse shall be carried first into the church, that is to be buried in the churchyard; and whether it shall be buried before the sermon, reading, or prayer, or after, or in the midst of reading; or whether any prayer shall be made at the grave for the living: let no Christians uncharitably judge one another about these things. Let no people keep up groundless usages, that being suspicious, grieve their minister, and offend their brethren. Let no minister that scrupleth the satisfying of people's ungrounded desires in such things, be forced to do it against his conscience; and let ministers that do use (any of) these customs or ceremonies, have liberty, when they suspect the people desire them upon some error, to profess against that error, and teach the people better.
>
> Whether the minister come with the company that brings the corpse from the house, or whether he meet them or receive them at the burial-place, is to be left to his own discretion. But while he is with them let him gravely discourse of man's mortality, and the useful truths and duties thence to be inferred. And either at the grave, or in the reading-place, or pulpit, by way of sermon, according to his

discretion, let him (at least, if it be desired) instruct and exhort the people concerning death, and the life to come, and their necessary preparation; seeing the spectacle of mortality, and the season of mourning, do tend to prepare men for a sober, considerate entertainment of such instructions. And he may read such Scriptures as may remind them of death, resurrection, and eternal life; as I Corinthians xv., or from verse 10 to the end; and Job i.21 and xix.25, 26, 27; John xi.25, 26 and v. 28, 29. And his prayer shall be suited to the occasion.

Whenever the rain, snow, or coldness of the season make it unhealthful to the minister or people to stand out of doors, at least let the reading, exhortation and prayers, be used within the church.[43]

At the Savoy Conference the Presbyterians failed to win more than a few minor concessions from the bishops, and the Prayer Book which was issued the following year contained many alterations of which they disapproved. There were a few changes in the burial service. A rubric was added at the beginning stating that 'the Office ensuing is not to be used for any that die unbaptized, or excommunicate, or have laid violent hands upon themselves'. The old first rubric of 1552 was re-written to make it clear that it was 'the Priest and Clerks' that were to meet the cortège at the churchyard entrance, and not just the priest alone. Two psalms, xxxix, *Dixi custodiam*, and xc, *Domine, refugium*, were added after the opening sentences with the rubric that one or both of them were to be said 'after they are come into the Church'. After the psalm the lesson is to be read, thus restoring the pattern of the office of the dead section of the 1549 order of burial. In the *Media vita* the text is brought into harmony with the original by replacing the strange 'shutte not vp thy mercifull eyes to oure prayers' with 'shut not thy merciful Eares to our prayer'. In the prayer 'Almighty God, with whom do live the spirits of them that depart . . .' there are some slight alterations: instead of 'in whome the soules of them that be elected' 1661 reads '*with* whom the souls of *the faithful*'. In the final prayer 'Saint' is inserted before Paul in the collect, and 'The grace of our Lord Jesus Christ, &c.' is said at the end of the service, a suggestion put forward by bishop Cosin.[44]

Anglican and Free Church services, 1662–1928

There were no major changes in the pattern of the Prayer Book office until modern times, though proposals made in 1689 for amending the Prayer Book included some relating to the Burial service. No reference was to be made to God's accomplishing the number of his elect; 'it hath pleased thee to deliver this our brother' was deleted in favour of 'it hath pleased thee to instruct us in this heavenly knowledge'; I Thessalonians iv.13–17 was proposed as an alternative lesson to that from I Corinthians xv, to be used 'in colder or later seasons'; and instead of the phrase 'in sure and certain hope', the words 'in a firm belief of the resurrection of the dead at the last day in which they who die in the Lord shall rise again to eternal life through our Lord Jesus Christ' were to be substituted.[45]

The Prayer Book rite influenced a number of later Free Church rites, particularly those of the Methodists, though a number of alterations were made in it, usually along similar lines to the Presbyterian objections at the Savoy Conference. *The Sunday services of Methodists with other occasional services*, which appeared in 1786, contained a shortened version of the burial rite, in which the first rubric concerning the unbaptized, excommunicate, and suicides was removed; the committal sentence and preceding rubric were omitted; the prayer 'Almighty God' was deleted; and the phrase 'as our hope is this our brother doth' was cut out of the collect.[46] The Methodist practice of singing hymns at funerals was noted as a special characteristic.[47] All burials which took place in parish church-yards had, however, to be conducted according to the Prayer Book, though occasionally interment took place in silence with the Dissenting minister in attendance or presiding. Because the great majority of burials did take place in churchyards, this requirement of using the Anglican service became a point of contention between Anglicans and Nonconformists, though Nonconformist opposition was not so much concentrated on the service itself as on what they saw as Establishment privilege preventing them from ministering to their dead as they saw fit. It was more a political than a theological issue, though Anglican incumbents were undoubtedly nervous about the 'enthusiastic' character of some Nonconformist burials. The tension was not finally resolved until the passing of the Burials Act in 1880 allowed services other than the Prayer Book one to be held in churchyards, providing that they were Christian and orderly, and no address was given which was contemptuous of the Christian religion or of the ministers of another denomination.[48] A consequence of the Act was that many Nonconformists wished to show that they were capable of holding dignified burial services and drew them up accordingly. The English Presbyterians used either the *Euchologion* which had been compiled in Scotland in 1867 (to which G. W. Sprott, who had revived the custom of holding burial services in Scotland, had contributed), or else the Congregational rite devised by H. Allon, until the time when the revised *Westminster Directory* appeared in 1898.[49] In 1864 the Wesleyans had agreed that burial should be conducted according to liturgical forms, and in 1882 *The Book of Public Prayers and Services for the use of the people called Methodists* was issued. The burial rite in this retained the Prayer Book committal, unlike the 1786 order, but altered the wording to 'Forasmuch as it hath pleased Almighty God to call hence the soul of our dear brother here departed, we therefore commit his body to the ground in the sure and certain hope that the dead in Christ shall rise to everlasting life'. The United Methodist book closely resembled *The Book of Public Prayers*, and the *Book of Services for the use of the Bible Christian Church* contained a modified Prayer Book rite, with a slight alteration in the words of committal: 'to take unto Himself the soul of our dear brother here departed'. The *Book of Common Prayer revised according to the use of the Free Church of England* (1876) substituted 'take out of this world' for 'take unto himself'.[50]

Other Free Church rites were further from the Prayer Book order. A Baptist service is found in C. P. Gould and J. H. Shakespeare's *A Manual for Free-Church Ministers*, published in 1905. This begins with a series of sentences from the New Testament, after which may follow an address and a hymn, and then a prayer, which may be either extempore or according to a set form. The one provided runs as follows:

Almighty and most merciful Father, we draw near unto thee, the Fountain of all life and peace, that we may take shelter as beneath the shadow of thy wing. We are in the midst of change and decay, but thou changest not and thy years know no end. Thou hast spoken unto us those words of eternal life, which alone can give peace at this time. Therefore we look up to thee in this hour of bereavement and sorrow, that we may find strength in our weakness, light in our darkness and comfort in our grief.

We bless thee for him who is the resurrection and the life to all his people and who has brought life and immortality to light through his holy gospel. We give thee thanks that when thou dost call thy servants away, it is that they may be with thee where thou art, that they may behold thy glory.

We beseech thee to comfort those that mourn through the glorious hope inspired by thy word, and to grant that the lessons of sorrow may be learned, and the mystery of thy loving discipline. (Here fitting and particular reference to the deceased and the bereaved may be made.)

Be with us all. Strengthen us for all that we have to bear or to accomplish. Cleanse our hearts by the blood of Jesus. Grant to us a part in those things which death cannot remove, and prepare us for the great change, that so we may through thy mercy enter into the everlasting rest and recompense through Jesus Christ our Lord.

The Lord's Prayer is then said. At the grave there are further sentences beginning with the opening words of the *Media vita*, and continuing with the last of the opening sentences of the Prayer Book rite. There is a modified form of the committal sentence, and then an optional prayer of thanksgiving for the redemption and assurance known in Christ and petition for the strengthening and sanctification of the living, followed by a prayer for the bereaved, 'The peace of God, &c.' and the grace. Two hymns are suggested as especially suitable: 'Come, let us join our friends above', and 'Peace, perfect peace'.[51] M. E. Aubrey's *A Minister's Manual* (1927) provides a service which follows much the same pattern.[52]

No new Anglican burial rite appeared until the Prayer Book revision of 1927–1928, but in the course of the nineteenth century there were many who pressed for changes in practice. The *Book of Common Prayer Revised* (1873) and the *Protestant Prayer Book* (1894), both of which were unofficial revisions made by the Evangelical wing of the Church, made three alterations: a change in the committal to read 'to take out of this world the soul of our dear brother here departed'; the omission of 'We give thee hearty thanks, for that it hath pleased thee to deliver this our brother out of the miseries of this sinful world'; and the leaving out of the phrase 'as our hope is this our brother doth'.[53] In a very different way the liturgical and patristic interests fostered by the Tractarians and the Cambridge Ecclesiologists led to demands for prayers for the dead and funeral eucharists. In 1853 the *Ecclesiologist* complained that there was no eucharist at the funeral of the archbishop of Sydney, and the same journal, in its recommendations for model cemeteries, proposed resident cemetery chaplains to provide for the celebration of requiem eucharists.[54] Bishop Christopher Wordsworth in 1872 appears to have been the first Anglican bishop to allow requiem celebrations officially, followed ten years later by bishop Mackarness, and in 1896 by the ruling of the bishop of Salisbury in synod that the clergy might celebrate them 'as the need arose'.[55] The Ecclesiologists endeavoured to recover some of the traditional medieval appurtenances, which they believed to be part of true Christian funerals, and attacked what they described as 'mere undertakery' and 'sepulchral haberdashery'. 'The high tomb, the coped coffin, the brass, the cross, the effigy, the chantry chapel', were what they hoped to see restored, and they were in a measure successful. Some of the burial guilds which were formed had as their object, not only the necessary insurance to cover the cost of the funeral and to make the arrangements for burial, but also the ordering of the funeral itself in what was considered to be a truly Christian manner. Such was the guild begun in Stoke Newington in 1850 by Robert Brett, which urged, amongst other things, the celebration of the eucharist at funerals if the deceased was a communicant.[56] The Guild of All Souls was founded in 1873 with the twofold object of providing funeral furniture (biers, palls, &c.) 'according to the use of the Catholic Church' and to set forth the doctrines of the Communion of Saints and the Resurrection of the Body, and intercessory prayer for the dying and for the repose of the souls of the departed. A requiem was held for Queen Victoria in 1901.[57] Prayer for the dead and requiem celebrations of the eucharist would not, however, have become as widely established as they did in Anglican practice, had it not been for the effect of the First World War, when they were often found to answer a need which no other forms appeared to do.

The revised Burial Service of the 1928 Prayer Book returned more to the pattern of the 1549 book, partly as a result of these changed attitudes. New rubrics were added at the beginning. The prohibitions on the use of the office were extended from suicides and excommunicates to those dying 'in the act of committing any grievous crime', and the bishop was to judge if there was any dispute concerning the use of the office in any particular instance. Six additional opening sentences were added, and the rubric before changed to permit only one sentence to be said and one or more of the Penitential Psalms. Psalms xxiii and cxxx were added to the psalmody in the church service, and rubrics were added permitting the response 'Rest eternal grant unto them, O Lord' to be said after each psalm, and the anthem 'O Saviour of the world, who by thy Cross and precious Blood hath redeemed us: Save us and help us we humbly beseech thee, O Lord' to be said before or after any psalm or group of psalms. Alternative lessons (II Corinthians iv. 16–v.10; Revelation vii.9–17; and Revelation xxi.1–7) were provided. Psalm ciii.13–17 is offered as an alternative to the burial anthems at the grave. There is an alternative prayer of committal, which is a slightly altered version of the prayer 'We commend into thy hands of mercy' in the 1549 book. The sentence 'Now unto the King eternal, immortal, invisible, the only wise God, be honour and glory for ever and ever. Amen', is given as a possible addition to the sentence, 'I heard a voice from heaven'. The ancient responses (*Non intres in iudicium*, &c.) were restored after the Lord's prayer, including a specific petition for the departed, 'Grant unto him eternal rest: And let perpetual light shine upon him.' Three new prayers were provided at the end of the service, one for light and peace for the departed, and the working of God's purpose in them; one for the mourners; and one for the strengthening of faith in 'the Communion of saints, the forgiveness of sins, and the resurrection to life everlasting'. Propers are also provided for a funeral Eucharist, the Epistle and the Gospel being those of the 1560 Latin Prayer Book, from which is also derived the use of the collect, 'O merciful God', from the Burial Service as the collect of the Funeral Eucharist. II Corinthians iv.16–v.4 is provided as an alternative epistle. A prayer for the blessing of a grave in unconsecrated ground and rubrics providing for the necessary alternations in wording for a cremation were added at the end. A whole new order for the burial of a child was placed immediately after the burial rite proper, whose pattern it follows with differences in the lesson and in some of the prayers.

The 1928 Prayer Book thus provided Anglicans in the alternatives it offered with a richer burial rite than they had had since 1549, even though the book was never authorised by Parliament. Yet, despite the changes and additions, the rite does not reflect the primitive awareness that the rite of burial was to be linked with both the Easter gospel and the Christian's baptism into the death and resurrection of Christ. That emphasis is only just beginning to be realized in Western Christianity as a result of the Liturgical Movement.

6 *The Christian funeral in a contemporary context*

Christian burial rites have varied from extended services intended to sanctify the whole range of actions from the moment of death to the completion of the act of burial, to rites, if they can be described as such, in which the only significant action has been the burial itself conducted without prayers. The concerns most evident in the prayers have ranged from a commendation of the departed to God, through prayers for mercy and deliverance from the torments of hell or the terrors of the Day of Judgment, to admonitions to the living to lead virtuous lives in the face of death which strikes at the root of human pride. In course of time the rites have been influenced by Jewish custom, by pagan practice (both by assimilation and rejection), and by the special conditions prevailing in monastic houses. They have been shaped at various times by different theologies, one emphasizing the perfecting of baptism and participation in the paschal mystery of the Lord's own death and resurrection, another stressing the need for deliverance from punishment and the necessary purification of the sinner.

The Revised Roman Rite

Contemporary revisions of the burial rite have brought many of the different traditions closer to each other, largely through a return to the more positive early theology with its emphasis on baptism and the resurrection, though prayers for the dead still remain a difficult area in which to reach theological agreement.[1] The Second Vatican Council set out clearly in its Constitution on the Sacred Liturgy the norms which were to be followed in the revision of the Roman rite of burial:

81. The rite for the burial of the dead should evidence more clearly the paschal character of Christian death, and should correspond more closely to the circumstances and traditions found in various regions. The latter provision holds good also for the liturgical colour to be used.

The revised Funeral Rite approved by the Bishops' Conference for use in England and Wales in 1971 shows how this has been worked out in practice.[2]

The rite consists of four sections (five, if the body is brought to the church at some earlier time), namely the Funeral Mass, the Final Commendation and Farewell, The Procession to the Grave, and the service at the graveside. The Reception of the Funeral Procession may take place immediately before the beginning of the Mass, in which case it consists of a prayer that 'the soul of your servant *N*, whom you have called from this life, may be brought by you to a place of peace and light, and so be enabled to share the life of all your saints', together with a responsory, such as that based on Job, 'I know that my Redeemer lives'. Or it may be a separate service, held earlier, at which there is a reading of the Gospel (John xiv. 1–6); a psalm (cxvi, *Dilexi quoniam*, which we have noted as one of the oldest psalms associated with burial); and the Lord's Prayer. The Entry Antiphon of the Mass is 'Lord, grant that they may have eternal rest, and be for ever in the radiance of your light', and the Responsorial Psalm, recited as the Gradual, is Psalm xxiii, though alternative series of responses and Alleluias are also provided. The Bidding Prayers begin with a specifically paschal and baptismal reference:

Priest: Let us call trustingly upon God the Almighty Father, who raised Christ his Son from the dead, for the salvation of the living and the dead.

Reader: Our brother (sister) *N* received in his (her) baptism the seed of eternal life. May he (she) enjoy the company of the saints for ever.

The Final Commendation and Farewell, which may take place either at the graveside or in church immediately after the end of the Mass, begins with an exhortation by the priest.

It is our solemn duty to carry out, in the traditional manner of God's faithful people, the burial of this mortal body. As we do so, we call trustfully upon God from whom all creation has life. May he in due time, by his power, bring to resurrection with all the saints, the body of this our brother (sister), which in its frailty we now bury. May God unite his (her) soul with those of all the saints and faithful departed. May he (she) be given a merciful judgment, so that redeemed from death, freed from punishment, reconciled to the Father, carried in the arms of the Good Shepherd, he (she) may deserve to enter fully into everlasting happiness in the company of the eternal King together with all the saints.

After a period of silent prayer, the *Subvenite* is said and a prayer of commendation petitioning that 'the gates of paradise may be opened' to the departed in 'the sure hope that he, together with all who have died in Christ, will rise again with Christ on the last day.' The body is then carried from the church to the antiphons *In paradisum* and *Chorus angelorum*, and the sentence 'I am the resurrection and the life'.

The third section, the Funeral Procession to the grave, consists only of Psalm cxviii, *Confitemini Domino*, with the antiphon *Aperite mihi portas*, 'Open for me the gates of righteousness'. This is another ancient text, being found at this point in the order in the Cologne MS. 123. At the graveside there is first a prayer for the blessing of the grave, if this is necessary, and then the grave and the body are sprinkled with holy water and censed. The body is lowered into the grave and a prayer of committal and commendation is said. A bidding prayer for the departed follows, with reference to the Lord's raising of the dead to life and his promise of paradise to the penitent thief, and to the participation of the departed in Baptism and the Eucharist. The rite concludes with the Lord's Prayer; a final prayer for mercy for the departed that 'as he was united in the true faith with all your faithful people', so now he may be 'united with the angelic throng'; and the response, 'Eternal rest grant to him, O Lord: And let light perpetual shine upon him.'

A somewhat different revision of the Roman rite is found in the experimental funeral rite authorized for use in the archdiocese of Chicago.[3] This has three main divisions, a Wake Service, a Church Service, and a short graveside rite. The Wake service consists of a reading from scripture, psalms, and responses; possibly a short homily; the Lord's Prayer, and the Prayer of the Faithful. This takes place in the mortuary chapel, in accordance with American practice. When the body is brought to the church the paschal and baptismal note is struck immediately. The funeral procession is met at the church door by the priest vested in white, accompanied by servers carrying the processional cross and the paschal candle. The coffin is sprinkled with holy water—a ceremony specifically linked with baptism by the reading of Romans vi. 3–5; the coffin is then covered with a white pall, again symbolizing the white robes of the newly baptised. The funeral mass then takes place, followed by the Final Commendation and a simple litany in place of the *Libera me*. The procession to the grave is led by the cross and the paschal candle. At the grave there is a short gospel reading, a psalm, a brief litany and the Lord's Prayer. There is no *Benedictus* as in the old rite.

What is notable about both these revisions is their simplicity and clarity of order, together with their prayers which look forward to the presence of God and the fullness of the communion of saints, on the basis of the sacramental sharing in baptism in the death and resurrection of Christ. The notes of fear and punishment have largely disappeared, and earlier forms have been drawn upon rather than the late medieval material, such as the *Dies Irae*. Indeed, so strongly does the note of paschal joy and triumph come through in the Chicago rite that it has been questioned whether it does not fail in its recognition of the pain and grief of death, which must also be part of a realistic Christian understanding. A balance has to be struck so that the liturgy of committal is 'at once triumphant and penitential, confident and suppliant, exultant and restrained'.[4]

Some Anglican Revisions

The recently revised burial offices of the Church of England, now published under the title of 'Funeral Services', are still considerably influenced by the Prayer Book tradition, and the sombre notes in general continue to predominate. By contrast the new burial services of the Episcopal Church in America draw on a wider range of traditional liturgy and are much more clearly marked by the Easter joy and hope that characterized the funeral liturgies of the early church. It is instructive to compare the comments of the Church of England Liturgical Commission on the purpose of the burial service in its report *Alternative Services* (*Second Series*), published in 1965, with the preface to 'An Order for Burial' in the *Proposed Book of Common Prayer* of the Episcopal Church (1976). The English Liturgical Commission write that the burial service has a fivefold purpose:

(*a*) To secure the reverent disposal of the corpse; (*b*) To commend the deceased to the care of our heavenly Father; (*c*) To proclaim the glory of our risen life in Christ here and hereafter; (*d*) To remind us of the awful certainty of our own coming death and judgment: (*e*) To make plain the eternal unity of Christian people, living and departed, in the risen and ascended Christ.[5]

The preface to the 'Order for Burial' reads:

The liturgy for the dead is an Easter liturgy. It finds all its meaning in the resurrection. Because Jesus was raised from the dead, we, too, shall be raised.

The liturgy, therefore, is characterized by joy. This joy, however, does not make human grief unchristian. The very love we have for each other in Christ brings deep sorrow when we are parted at death. Jesus himself wept at the grave of his friend. So, while we rejoice that one we love has entered into the nearer presence of our Lord, we sorrow in sympathy with those who mourn.[6]

The Episcopalian orders model the first part of the burial liturgy on the liturgy of the Word in the Eucharist; clear provision is made for the celebration of the Eucharist by a rubric following the Gospel or Creed, whereas the English revisions still print in a separate section the directions for a funeral at which there is a celebration of the Eucharist; and a comparison of the prayers of commendation in the English and American orders shows that the latter are both more direct and closer to the ethos of the early Christian liturgies. The accompanying table (pp. 104–8) sets out the proposed English revision of 1965, which did not gain general approval; the authorized 'Series III' revision; and the draft Episcopalian proposals.

Some of the prayers and anthems suggested in the Episcopalian order, which were too long to be included in the table, are worth noting. In section 10, the Prayers, the two litany forms provided have much to commend them.

The following extracts are given as examples:

Grant that all who have been baptized into Christ's death and resurrection may die to sin and rise to newness of life, and that through the grave and gate of death we may pass with him to our joyful resurrection. *Amen.*

Grant to us who are still in our pilgrimage, and who walk as yet by faith, that thy Holy Spirit may lead us in holiness and righteousness all our days. *Amen.*

Grant us, with all who have died in the hope of the resurrection, to have our consummation and bliss in thy eternal and everlasting

Three Anglican revisions of the burial rites

Series II (1965 proposals)	Series III	Episcopalian prayer book (1976)
1. Funeral Sentences Six N.T. passages, three from John, three from Romans. (Job xix. 25 omitted as based on a mistranslation; John xi. 25, 26 opening sentence).	**Funeral Sentences** Nine N.T. and O.T. passages. (Job xix. 25 omitted; John xi. 25, 26 obligatory opening sentences.)	**Funeral Sentences** Four passages, 3 N.T., 1 O.T. (Job xix. 25); John xi. 25, 26 opening sentence. *Or* (in the Second Order) a version of the *Media Vita* with the response, *'Holy God, Holy and mighty, Holy and merciful Saviour, deliver us not into the bitterness of eternal death'*.
2.	**Opening Collect** Prayer (from 1928 order) 'that we may live as those who believe in the communion of saints, the forgiveness of sins, and the resurrection to eternal life'.	**Opening Collect** Preceded by greeting. 3 alternative prayers provided: (*a*) 'that your servant *N*, being raised with (Christ), may know the strength of his presence, and rejoice in his eternal glory.' (*b*) 'Accept our prayers on behalf of your servant *N*, and grant *him* an entrance into the land of light and joy, in the fellowship of your saints.' (*c*) 'we remember before you this day our brother (sister) *N*. We thank you for giving *him* to us, *his* family and friends, to know and to love as a companion on our earthly pilgrimage. In your boundless compassion, console us who mourn. Give us faith to see in death the gate of eternal life, so that in quiet confidence we may continue our course on earth, until, by your call, we are reunited with those who have gone before.'
3.		*The Liturgy of The Word* **Old Testament Lesson** Isaiah xxv. 6–9; Isaiah lxi. 1–3; Lamentations iii. 22–6, 31–33; Wisdom iii. 1–5, 9. The Second Order includes also Job xix. 21–27a.

4. *Psalmody*
cxxxix. 1–9 (compulsory); xc; xxiii; cxxi; cxxx.

5. *Lesson*
I Corinthians xv (abbreviated).

6.

7.

8. *Sermon* (optional)

9. *Nunc dimittis*

10. *The Prayers*
Kyrie (three fold)
Lord's Prayer
Media vita
(3rd part: 'Thou knowest, Lord, the secrets of our hearts')

Psalmody
xxiii; xc (abbreviated); cxxi; cxxx. Other suggested: verses from xxvii; cxviii; cxxxix.

Lesson
John xiv. 1–10; I Corinthians xv (abbreviated); I Thessalonians iv. 13–18.

Sermon (optional)
Te Deum Pt. II

The Prayers
Kyrie (three fold)
Lord's Prayer
Optional prayers

Psalmody
xlii; xlvi; xc; cxxi; cxxx; cxxxix (suggested as appropriate; may be replaced by a hymn or canticle).

New Testament Lesson
Romans viii. 14–39 (abbreviated); I Corinthians xv (abbreviated); II Corinthians iv. 16–v. 9; I John iii. 1–2; Revelation vii. 9–17; xxi. 2–7.

Canticle, Hymn or Psalmody
Suggested psalms xxiii; xxvii; cvi. 1–5; cxvi.

Gospel
John v. 24–27; vi. 37–40; x. 11–16; xi. 21–27; xiv. 1–6.

Sermon (optional)

Creed (optional)
Introduced in the second order by the words: 'In the assurance of eternal life given at Baptism, let us proclaim our faith and say,....'

The Prayers
Two litany forms are provided.

Three Anglican revisions of the burial rites—contd.

Series II (1965 proposals)	Series III	Episcopalian prayer book (1976)
Collect	*Collect*	
(A shortened version of the Prayer Book Collect, 'O merciful God, the Father of our Lord Jesus Christ', asking that God will 'raise us from the death of sin unto the life of righteousness: that when we shall depart this life we may with this our *brother* be found acceptable unto thee.')	('Grant us, Lord, the wisdom and the grace to use aright the time that is left to us here on earth. Lead us to repent of our sins, the evil we have done and the good we have not done: and strengthen us to follow the steps of your Son, in the way that leads to the fullness of eternal life.')	
	Hymn (optional)	
11. *Optional prayers*		
12. *The Commendation*	*The Commendation*	*The Commendation*
'Let us commend our *brother N* into the hands of God, our maker and redeemer.'	'Let us commend our *brother N* to the mercy of God our Maker and Redeemer.'	Kontakion for the departed, 'Give rest, O Christ, to your servant(s) with the saints'.
'O God, our heavenly Father, who by thy mighty power hast given us life, and by thy lovingkindness hast bestowed upon us new life in Christ Jesus: We commend to thy merciful keeping thy servant *N* our *brother* here departed.'	'Heavenly Father, by your mighty power you have given us new life in Christ Jesus. We entrust *N* to your merciful keeping: in the faith of Jesus Christ your Son our Lord.'	'Into your hands, O merciful Savior, we commend your servant *N.* Acknowledge, we humbly beseech you, a sheep of your own fold, a lamb of your own flock, a sinner of your own redeeming. Receive *him* into the arms of your mercy, into the blessed rest of everlasting peace, and into the glorious company of the saints in light.'

Dismissal

Optional anthems or a hymn or canticles.

'May God in his infinite love and mercy bring the whole Church, living and departed in the Lord Jesus, to a joyful resurrection and the fulfilment of his eternal kingdom.'

The Committal

Anthems

Media vita (First order): John vi. 37, Romans viii. 11, Psalm xvi. 9, 11 (Second order—optional alternative in the First).

Committal Prayer

('In sure and certain hope of the resurrection to eternal life through our Lord Jesus Christ, we commend to Almighty God our *brother N*, and we commit *his* body to the ground; earth to earth, ashes to ashes, dust to dust. The Lord bless *him* and keep *him*, the Lord make his face to shine upon *him* and be gracious to *him*, the Lord lift up his countenance upon *him* and give *him* peace'.)

Lord's Prayer

Rest eternal grant to *him*, O Lord...

May *his* soul, and the souls of all the departed, through the mercy of God, rest in peace. (optional)

'Unto the King eternal, immortal, invisible...'

13. *The Committal*

Psalm ciii. 8, 13–17 (optional)

The Committal

Sentence (Revelation xiv. 13, *Audivi vocem*) (optional)

Either Psalm cii. 8, 13–17 *or* 'Man born of woman has but a short time to live' and the *Media vita*.

13. *Committal Prayer*

'Forasmuch as our *brother N* has departed out of this life: We therefore commit *his* body (*or* ashes) to the ground; earth to earth, ashes to ashes, dust to dust; having our whole trust and confidence in the mercy of our heavenly Father, and in the victory of his son, Jesus Christ our Lord...'

Committal Prayer

('We have entrusted our *brother N* to God's merciful keeping, and we now commit *his* body to the ground...earth to earth, ashes to ashes, dust to dust; in sure and certain hope of the resurrection to eternal life through our Lord Jesus Christ').

Three Anglican revisions of the burial rites—contd.

Series II (1965 proposals)	Series III	Episcopalian prayer book (1976)
14. *Dismissal* 'May the God of peace, who brought again from the dead...'	*Dismissal* Sentence. Psalm xvi. 11 'Unto him that is able to keep us from falling...' (Jude 24, 25)	*Dismissal* Response ('Alleluia. Christ is risen. *The Lord is risen indeed. Alleluia.* Let us go forth in the name of Christ. *Thanks be to God.*') 'The God of peace, who brought again from the dead...'

glory, and, with (blessed *N* and) all thy saints, to receive the crown of life which thou dost promise to all who share in the victory of thy Son Jesus Christ...*Amen.*[7]

For our brother (sister) *N*, let us pray to our Lord Jesus Christ who said, 'I am Resurrection and I am Life'.

Lord, you consoled Martha and Mary in their distress; draw near to us who mourn for *N*, and dry the tears of those who weep. *Hear us, Lord.*

You raised the dead to life; give to our brother (sister) eternal life.
Hear us, Lord.

He was nourished with your Body and Blood; grant *him* a place at the table in your heavenly kingdom. *Hear us, Lord.*[8]

In the anthems provided at the end of the commendation (section 12) as the body is borne from the church, the Easter note of resurrection is clearly stressed:

Christ is risen from the dead, trampling down death by death, and giving life to those in the tomb.

The Sun of Righteousness is gloriously risen, giving light to those who sat in darkness and in the shadow of death.

The Lord will guide our feet into the way of peace, having taken away the sin of the world.

Christ will open the kingdom of heaven to all who believe in his Name, saying, Come, O blessed of my Father; inherit the kingdom prepared for you.

Into paradise may the angels lead you. At your coming may the martyrs receive you, and bring you into the holy city Jerusalem.[9]

There is thus a clear structure in this order with the body being brought into church, or the funeral service beginning, with the series of sentences expressing both Christian hope and human need and sorrow in death, and ending, after the reading of scripture, and prayer, and possibly the celebration of the Eucharist, with Easter affirmations. That note is muted in the English revisions, though if some of the additional prayers provided are used it would sound more clearly.

Both the Series III English revision and the Episcopalian proposals include short vigil services. The Series III order consists of a sentence; a lesson (Romans viii. 31b–39); psalms (xxvii. 1–8; cxxxix. 1–11, 17–18); the Lord's Prayer; additional prayers and the grace. The Episcopalian order has the rubric that 'it is appropriate that the family and friends come together for prayers prior to the funeral. Suitable Psalms, Lessons, and Collects may be used. The Litany at the Time of Death may be said', or an alternative litany of commendation, which is provided, with the response: *Into your hands, O Lord, we commend our brother (sister) N.* The provision of such services, and the fuller provision in the Episcopalian Draft Prayer Book for Ministration at the time of Death, can only be welcomed.

The Funeral rite as pastoral Liturgy

The breakdown of traditional mourning customs, and the conspiracy of silence about death and dying, means that there is a greater, not a lesser, need for proper provision to be made for words to be said and things to be done, to enable the bereaved to cope with the pain and loss of death, and for the dying to be given the assurance and hope to face it. The early Church, in a society where the care of the dying and the burial of the dead was still a common responsibility, was able to take the necessary actions of preparing the body for burial, bearing it to the burial ground, and laying it in the grave, and surround them with prayers and ceremonies which made it clear that this last journey was the symbol of the more significant journey of man's home-coming to God. As the liturgy of burial changed and developed through the Christian centuries, the hallowing of these actions, and the setting of them in a Christian context, gave way to meditations on mortality, moralizing on the virtues of the departed, and seizing the occasion of death to issue solemn warnings to the living. The effect of the Reformation was, amongst other things, to remove many of the traditional symbolic acts of piety, with the consequence that mourning customs came to have scant Christian content, and were frequently little more than the opportunity for the parade of secular rank. Feathers, mutes, and the yards of black crape that characterized Victorian funerals were rightly attacked by Christian funeral reformers as having no meaning or significance for the Christian understanding of death, but the result of the abandonment of the mourning rituals of the nineteenth century is that our secular society is left without mourning rituals at all.[10] Mourning is important, for Christians as well as for non-Christians. There is plenty of evidence of the psychological damage caused by suppressed grief. Any burial liturgy must be framed to help this process. It must neither be death-denying, nor death-defying, for both are in the end escape-routes from the reality of death and separation which must be recognized and lived through. This has been well put by Edgar Jackson, when he writes: 'The wisely conducted funeral service helps preserve the freedom of the future by creating the atmosphere for wisely letting go of the past.' It must help the work of grieving, in which 'the change wrought by death must be accepted in order wisely to recall the life that was'.[11]

The age of specialism in which we live has meant that even the nineteenth-century situation, when death frequently occurred in the midst of the family, let alone the situation of earlier generations and simpler societies where a death was shared in by the whole community, is no longer the context of death. Today, as John Hick has well put it, 'death instead of being perforce everybody's business has been taken over by specialists—the physician, the funeral director, the clergyman'.

> 'This institutionalization of death, whilst it brings the resources of medical science to bear in aid of the dying, must also have the effect of reinforcing our cultural taboo upon death. An event that takes place under sedation in the privacy of a curtained hospital bed can the more easily be kept behind psychological curtains as something that is not talked about.'[12]

But when a death has occurred it must be talked about, if it is to be accepted, and the burial liturgy of the Church must provide a way of talking about death which is realistic, marking the separation which has taken place, and which yet offers a genuinely Christian assurance of the sustaining power of God, who is the Lord and Giver of life. The feelings of anger and guilt that the bereaved may have need to be recognized by those pastorally involved with the funeral and the care of the bereaved afterwards. Liturgically this means that a stress on the commendation of the departed to God, coupled with an unsentimental assurance of the forgiveness and love of the God to whom the departed is commended, are of clear importance.

In her recent book *Death and the Family* Lily Pincus stresses again and again the ways in which bereavement can lay bare the anxieties and failures of relationships which are now, through a death, in the past: the crisis of bereavement highlights the inner situation of the bereaved.[13] It can lead to regression, to infantile and irrational behaviour: 'it is not just losing a state in which one had found one's balance, but rather as if one has lost one's balanced self.'[14] It is imperative, therefore, that the rites of passage are not hurried and rushed. The bereaved need help 'to adjust from relating to the living to relating to the dead person, or to the change in her own status from a wife (husband) to a widow (widower).' 'Human beings need to mourn in response to loss, and if they are denied this, they will suffer, psychologically, physically, or both.'[15]

It is easier to diagnose the shortcomings of our society in this respect than to see clearly how the situation may be altered. But it is surely clear that the Church should not join the conspiracy of silence about death, and should encourage all those with whom it has contact to see the importance of facing both the fact of death and the needs of the bereaved. Professor Alasdair MacIntyre, amongst others, has suggested that the Church is failing to do this. Arguing that 'we cannot do with Christianity in the modern world, but often cannot do without it entirely either, because we have no other vocabulary in which to raise certain kinds of question', he applies this to 'our inability to respond to the facts of death.'

> I am not talking now about a simple intellectual ability to produce formulas in which we can say what we believe about death. I am talking about those situations in which we are forced to ask ourselves if in the face of actual deaths we can go on repeating these formulas. This is one of the great cultural and social gaps in our lives, but it is quite clear than in face of this particular crisis Christians have been in the same difficulty as everyone else... The fact is that contemporary Christianity says *nothing* about death.[16]

That, at least, is how it strikes one observer, and this is a theological challenge which must not be avoided. But there is also a pastoral challenge to help Christian believers to reflect on the fact of death—their own death and the deaths of others—and, by enabling them to draw on the resources of the Christian tradition, which is so firmly rooted in the resurrection faith and hope, to find ways of expressing that same faith and hope within the culture of our own day. Any Christian burial liturgy must reflect the fullness of that tradition, and use it creatively to minister to the needs of the bereaved. If, as a recent writer has said, 'the Christian minister is the one whose vocation it is to make it possible for man not only to fully face his human situation but also to celebrate it in all its awesome reality,' that celebration for the Christian 'is only possible through the deep realization that life and death are never found completely separate... When we celebrate a wedding, we celebrate a union as well as a departure, when we celebrate death we celebrate lost friendship as well as gained liberty.'[17] The Christian liturgy of burial must bear the character of just such a celebration.

In the traditional Eastern liturgies of burial the primitive Christian pattern and emphases have been more fully preserved than in the West. But urban society has had its effect in the East as well as in the West, and in practice the liturgy is considerably curtailed. In an age of rapid transport the lengthy accompanying chants of the funeral. procession have no place. In the West urbanization and technology have had their effect in another way—in the move from burial to cremation as the most common way of disposing of the bodies of the dead. The cities of Victorian England with their crowded population soon filled the parish churchyards with their dead, and scandal and irreverence resulted from the over-crowding. Municipal cemeteries were opened to resolve the problem; inevitably the cemeteries meant a further break in the connection between church and community. The churchyard had linked disposal of the dead with the worshipping community of the church; the cemetery linked it with 'the improvement of moral sentiments and general taste', an environment, it might be said, of didactic horticulture.[18] Cremation, as a way of disposing of the dead, is part of this same shift of emphasis. It began to be publicly advocated in the 1870s and the first crematoria in England were opened in the 1880s.[19] The Church was suspicious. Cremation was viewed by some as a pagan practice; by others, more literally minded, as creating difficulties for a faith committed to a doctrine of the resurrection of the body. For one reason or another, the Church tended to stand aside and the result has been that the character of crematoria, both architecturally and symbolically, has been determined outside a Christian frame of reference, even though some Christian symbolism may be employed. 'Cremation, in this country, is basically a secular arrangement to which religion has become attached', and the buildings reflect this ambiguity. They are churches which are not churches, often having altars which are never used as Christian altars. Moreover, the act of committal, the final and decisive farewell to the departed, which is their *raison d'être*, is obscured, because the disappearance of the coffin from view is not a true committal, parallel to the casting of earth on to a coffin in a grave. It has been forcefully argued that this is both psychologically and, for the Christian, theologically inappropriate.[20] Any funeral rite must take account of this situation and attempt to counter it, though the changes needed are as much architectural as liturgical.[21]

*　　*　　*

The history of the Christian liturgy for the dead makes it clear that there is a wealth of material to draw on as we seek in prayer and action to express the Christian hope. A fuller study of the Christian burial rites as they have developed historically would undoubtedly bring much more to light, and would enable, for instance, the text of particular prayers to be traced in detail. But this has not been the intention of this introductory survey. This has been limited to the more modest task of showing the general lines of development of the ways in which Christians have bidden farewell to those who have departed this life, describing and summarizing the various rites, and indicating something of the different theological understandings of the meaning of this farewell. Whatever the vicissitudes of liturgical change, the burial rite has always been the final seal placed on the life of the Christian, and a commendation into the hands of God, whether that commendation has taken the form of a triumphant celebration of a heavenly birthday, or a prayer for mercy and deliverance, or a trusting committal in a sure and certain hope of resurrection to eternal life.

Notes

Chapter 1

1. Matt. xxvii.59; Mk. xv.46; xvi.1; Lk. xxiii.53, 56; xxiv.1; Jn. xix.39–40. It has been suggested that the reference in Jn. xix.39 to a hundred pound weight of spice is excessive, and that the text should be emended to read ἕκαστον instead of ἑκατόν.
2. Jn. xx.7, cf. xi.44.
3. Acts v.6, 10.
4. Acts viii.2; ix.37, 39; cf. Mk. vi.38.
5. Lk. vii. 11–17.
6. Cf. also Tobit i.17–19.
7. TB. *Mo'ed Katan* 21a.
8. Ecclus. xxxviii.17; xxii.12.
9. Gen. 1.10 cf. *Pirkê de R. Eliezer* TB. *Semaḥoth* vii. For another argument cf. *Mo'ed Katan* 19b.
10. *Semaḥoth* viii.
11. *Semaḥoth* xi.
12. Ibid. xi.11; cf. TB. *Sanhedrin* 63a.
13. Ibid. xiv.
14. Josephus, BJ. II.i.1.
15. *Semaḥoth* ix.
16. TB. *Mo'ed Katan* 27; cf. *Kethuboth* 8b.
17. *Semaḥoth* vi (Soncino edn. p.351n.).
18. Cf. A. P. Bender, 'Beliefs, rites and customs of the Jews connected with death, burial and mourning', in *Jewish Quarterly Review*, VII (1894–1895), pp.101–118.
19. TB. b. *Bathra* 9a; *Sanhedrin* gives regulations for excess monies collected.
20. b. *Bathra* 100b.
21. TB. b. *Berakoth* 58a.
22. cf. J. Jeremias, *New Testament Theology*, I (1971), pp.198–199.
23. A. Z. Idelsohn, *Jewish Liturgy and its development*, New York 1932, p.87.
24. Jer. xxxii.19; Ps. xcii.15; Job i.21; Ps. lxxviii.38.
25. For English text of *Tzidduk Ha-din* cf. J. H. Hertz, *The Authorised Daily Prayer Book with Commentary* (1947), pp.1074ff.
26. J. M. C. Toynbee, *Death and Burial in the Roman World* (1971), p.41.
27. pp.43–64.
28. In Aristophanes' *Frogs* (138–140) Charon's fee is said to be two obols.
29. F. Cumont, *After Life in Roman Paganism* (1922), pp.50, 53.
30. Tertullian, *Apology* xiii.7; *De Test. Animae* iv.
31. *Apostolic Constitutions* viii.44.
32. Augustine, *Confessions* vi.
33. Cf. J. Quasten, '*Vetus superstitio et nova religio*: the problem of *Refrigerium* in the ancient church of North Africa', in *Harvard Theological Review* xxxiii (1940),

pp.253–266. For an account of the martyr-cult outside Africa, cf. E. Dyggve, *History of Salonitan Christianity*, Oslo 1951.

34. *Enchiridion* xxix.

35. *Ap. Const.* viii.42.

36. Cumont, p.53.

37. J. Jungmann, *The Early Liturgy* (1958), p.144.

38. Cumont, p.92.

39. *Ap. Const.* viii.42; Deut. xxxiv.8.

40. Cf. *Semaḥoth* vii; *Mo'ed Katan* 19b.

41. *De his qui in fide dormiunt* xv.

42. *De SS. Bernice et Prosdoce* iii.

43. *De vita Moesis* ii.281; iv.268; 8–14.

44. *Jubilees* xxiii.7.

45. E. Freistedt; *Altchristliche Totengedächtnistage und ihre Beziehung zum Jenseits-glauben und Totenkulten der Antike*, Münster 1928, p.4.

46. pp.51–52.

47. G. Grabka, 'Christian Viaticum: a study of its cultural background', in *Traditio* ix (1953), pp.1–43.

48. Cf. Grabka, pp. 28–30 for examples.

49. Justin Martyr, *Apology* I, 65, 67.

50. Canon xiii of the council forbids the dying to be deprived of 'the last and very necessary ἐφόδιον'.

51. *Historia Ecclesiastica.* vi.44. (cited afterwards as *HE*).

52. PG. 29.ccxv. q. Grabka. p.33; *Vita S. Melaniae* (early fifth century), 68.9, q. ibid. p.35.

53. Paulinus: *Life of Ambrose* x.

54. Canon xx. PL. 56, 882.

55. Cf. *Nicene and Post-Nicene Fathers*, xiv, pp.450–451. (cited afterwards as *N & PNF*.)

56. *Homily* 40 (*In ep. I ad Cor.*), PG. 61.347.

57. Grabka, p.42.

58. *Ep. ed Ephes.* xx.2.

59. Irenaeus, *Adv. Haer.* iv.18.5.

60. *Commentary on the Song of Songs.* PG. 44.989A.

61. Cited by P. M. Gy, 'La Mort du chrétien', in A. G. Martimart (ed.), *L'Église en Prière*, Tournai 1965³, p.637.

62. Ibid. pp.636–638.

63. Cf. the discussion of the theme of the voyage of life in Hugo Rahner, *Greek Myths and Christian Mystery* (1963), pp. 341–353.

64. Cf. e.g. Isaiah xi.7; xxxv.9; also the various legends of the obedience of lions in early monasticism.

65. Cited by H. Thurston, *The Memory of our dead* (1915), p.13.

66. P. S. Everts, *Hymni Mediaevales*, Zwolle 1950, p.29.

67. Gen. xxiv.7; Ex. xxiii.20; Numb. xx.16; Tobit v.4ff.

68. *Testament of Asher* vi.5–6.

69. J. Daniélou, *A History of Early Christian Doctrine*, I (The Theology of Jewish Christianity), (1964), p.187.

70. Tertullian: *De Anima* liii; Origen, *Homily on Numbers* v.4; *Commentary on Job* xix.4. q. J. Daniélou, *Les Anges et leur mission d'après les pères de l'Église* (Collection Irénikon, NS. 5), Gembloux 1952, pp.130–131.

71. E. Hennecke, *New Testament Apocrypha* ii, 1965, p.764.

72. H. A. Wilson, *The Gelasian Sacramentary*, Oxford 1894, p.298.

73. M. Magistretti, *Manuale Ambrosianum*, Milan 1905, I, pp.83, 65. Cf. the *Misericordiam tuam Domine sancte* in Beroldus, q. p.99.

74. *Ap. Const.* viii.41.

75. F. C. Conybeare & A. J. Maclean, *Rituale Armenorum*, Oxford 1905, p.127.

76. Mt. viii.11. There is reference in IV Maccabees xiii.17 to the Patriarchs receiving those who died in defence of the Law. TB. *Kiddushin* 72B has a probable reference to the bosom of Abraham. For further discussion of the phrase cf. Strack-Billerbeck, *Kommentar zum Neuen Testament aus Talmud und Midrash*, ii, Munich 1924, pp.225–227.

77. Gregory of Nyssa, *On the soul and resurrection*.

78. *Ep. ad Arsacium* xlix.

79. II Esdras ii.23. Oesterley suggests the reference to placing a sign may refer to the marking of the grave by a cross (*II Esdras*, 1933, p.13).

80. Augustine, *Care to be taken for the Dead* ii, iii.

81. Lactantius, *Divine Institutes* vi.12.

Chapter 2

1. *Apostolic Tradition* xxxiv.

2. *De Anima* li.

3. *Exhortation to chastity* xi; *De Monogamia* x. Cf. the later remark of St Ambrose: 'We pay no attention to the birthdays of the dead, but commemorate with great solemnity the day on which they died' (*De Excessu Satyri* ii.5).

4. Cyprian, *Letters* xii.2.

5. *Apology* xlii.

6. Prudentius, *Hymnus circa exequias defuncti*.

7. *HE.* VII.22.9.

8. *De vita Constantini* iv.66.

9. Ibid. iv.60, 71.

10. J. Wordsworth, *Bishop Serapion's Prayer Book* (1910[2]) pp.79–80.

11. *Apostolic Constitutions* vi.30; viii.41; F. E. Brightman, 'The Sacramentary of Serapion of Thmuis', *J.T.S.*, I (1900), p. 275.

12. E. Hennecke, *New Testament Apocrypha* I (1963), pp.415–416.

13. Jerome: *Ep.* cviii.30 (cvii.ii. PL. XXII.878).

14. *Ep.* xxvii.

15. Jerome, *Life of Paul the Hermit*, xvi.

16. *HE.* III.18. Cf. Sozomen, HE. V.19.

17. *Homily on Hebrews* iv.7.

18. *HE.* VII.46.

19. *Homily on John* lxii (on John xi.1–29); lxxxv.

20. Alfred C. Rush: 'The colors of black and red in the liturgy of the dead', in P. Granfield and J. A. Jungmann (eds.), *Kyriakon: Festschrift Johannes Quasten*, Münster 1970, ii, p.702.

21. *De Mort.* xx (CSEL. iii.309), q. Rush.

22. Basil, *De gratiae actione* vi.7 (PG. XXXI.229–233) q. Rush.

23. Ephraem Syrus, *Nisibene Hymns concerning Abraham, Bishop of Nisibis* xxi. (*N & PNF* xii. p.191).

24. *De consolatione mortis* ii.6. (PG. LVI.303) q. Rush.

25. *Funeral Oration on Meletius. N & PNF.* v. p.517; PG. XLVI.996ff.

26. *Ep.* cviii.30.

27. *Ep.* xxxix.

28. *Enarratio in Ps.* xxxiii (2),14.

29. *Confessions* ix.

30. Ibid.

31. Gregory the Great, *Ep.* ix.3 (*N & PNF.* XII. pp.1–2).

32. Hilary of Arles, *Sermo de vita Scti. Honorati* vii.

33. Chrysostom, *Hom. de dormit.* xxx.

34. R. H. Connolly (ed.), *Didascalia Apostolorum*, Oxford 1929, p.257 (Section xxvi).

35. *Apostolic Constitutions* vi.30.

36. q. Conybeare & Maclean, *Rituale Armenorum*, pp. 124, 126; R. M. Woolley, *Coptic Offices*, (1930) pp.110, 114, 117; cf. H. Frank, 'Die älteste *Ordo defunctorum* der Römischen Liturgie . . .', *Archiv für Liturgie-Wissenschaft* VII (1962).

37. In *Le Mystère de la Mort et sa Célébration* (Lex Orandi 12) Paris 1956, p.187n.

38. *Apostolic Constitutions* viii.41.

39. Ibid. viii.42, 43.

40. ET. and commentary by Denys Rutledge, *Cosmic Theology: The Ecclesiastical Hierarchy of Pseudo-Denys, an Introduction* (1964), pp.186–203.

41. Ibid. pp.188–189.

42. p.191.

43. p.189.

44. p.191–192.

45. p.199.

46. p.198. Cf. Theodore: *Penitential* II.v.1. 'Secundum Romanum ecclesiam mos est monachos vel homines religiosos defunctos aeclesiam portare, et cum crisma unguere pectora eorum, ibique pro eis missas celebrare; deinde cum cantatione portare ad sepulturas; et cum positi fuerint in sepulchro, funditur pro eis oratio deinde humo vel petra operiuntur.' (Text in A. W. Haddan & W. Stubbs, *Councils and Ecclesiastical Documents relating to Great Britain and Ireland* III, Oxford 1871, p.194). For the expanded version of the Penitential of Egbert on this point, cf. PL. LXXXIX.410. Haddan & Stubbs, III, pp.414–415, gives the history of the text.

47. II.v.8.

48. *Irénikon* I (1926), pp. 293–299.

Chapter 3

1. Woolley, *Coptic Offices*, pp.109–154; O.H.E. KHS-Burmester, *The Egyptian or Coptic Church, a detailed description of her liturgical services and the rites and ceremonies observed in the administration of her sacraments* (*Publications de la Société d'archéologie copte*), Cairo 1967, p.214.

2. Text in *ΕΥΧΟΛΟΓΙΟΝ ΤΟ ΜΕΓΑ* Venice, (1869) ('Ἀκολουθία νεκρώσιμος 'εἰς κόσμικος) pp.393ff. There is a not very satisfactory English translation in I. F. Hapgood, *Service Book of the Holy Orthodox-Catholic Apostolic (Greco-Russian) Church*, New York 1906, pp.369ff.

3. A hymn in honour of the Trinity.

4. Two *troparia* (short hymns) of which the first is preceded by $\Delta \acute{o} \xi \alpha$ $\Pi \acute{\alpha} \tau \rho \iota$ and the second by the $\kappa \alpha \grave{\iota}$ $\nu \hat{\nu} \nu$.

5. *Troparion* in honour of the Virgin.

6. *Troparia* sung whilst the community remain seated.

7. The *Kontakion* is the name given to the *troparion* of the Canon, which occurs at the end of the sixth ode, and is built on a *Hirmos* different from that of the ode itself. The *Kontakion* is followed by the *Ikos*, a hymn similar to a *troparion*, but of much greater length.

8. This occurs at Matins after the third division of the psalter of the day has been read, and it is composed on the basis of the gradual psalms.

9. *Troparion* composed on the basis of the Canon. On Sundays, for example, it comments on the Gospel of the Resurrection.

10. *Catechesis* xxiii.9.

11. Text in Conybeare & Maclean, *Rituale Armenorum*, pp.119–135. The text is basically that established by the Catholicos Mashtotz at the end of the ninth century.

12. Ibid. pp.243–268.

13. Ibid. p.253.

14. Burmester, pp.202ff.

15. Cf. text in F. E. Brightman, *Liturgies Eastern and Western* I, Oxford 1896, pp.148–149.

16. R.-G. Coquin, *Les Canons d'Hippolyte* (Patrologia Orientalis XXXI), Paris 1966, p. 405.

17. Roger Cowley, 'Attitudes to the Dead in the Ethiopian Orthodox Church', *Sobornost* VI.4 (1972), pp.241–256.

18. Roger Cowley, 'Parish Life in the Ethiopian Countryside', *Sobornost* V.3 (1966), p.199.

19. J. M. Harden, *An Introduction to Ethiopic Christian Literature* (1926), pp.22, 25.

20. J. M. Harden, *The Ethiopic Didascalia* (1920), p.166.

21. Cowley, 'Attitudes to the Dead', p. 253.

22. J. M. Harden: *The Anaphoras of the Ethiopic Liturgy* (1928), pp.97–98; E. Hammerschmidt, *Studies in the Ethiopic Anaphoras*, Berlin 1961, p.103.

23. Cowley, 'Attitudes to the Dead', p.246.

24. E. A. Wallis Budge, *The Bandlet of Righteousness: an Ethiopian Book of the Dead* (1929), p.63.

25. Ibid. p.76.

26. Cf. W. Macomber, 'The Funeral Liturgy of the Chaldean Church', *Concilium* II.iv (1968), pp.19–22.

27. Op.cit., II, pp.282–321.

28. A. P. Bender, 'Beliefs, rites and customs of the Jews connected with death, burial and mourning,' *Jewish Quarterly Review* VII (1894–1895), pp.101ff.

29. Isaac H. Hall, 'The Nestorian Ritual of Washing the Dead', *Hebraica* IV (1882), p.84.

30. Badger, op.cit., II, pp.315–316.

31. p.303n.

32. p.311n.

33. p.314, cf. Hall, p.85.

34. 'Office des funérailles et théologie de la mort d'après le manuscrit Vat. Syr. 59', *Proche-Orient Chrétien* XXIII (1973), pp.284–321.

35. J. Tabet, *L'Office des morts* (duplicated lectures given at the Institut Supérieur de Liturgie, Université Saint-Esprit, Kaslik, Lebanon, in 1970–1971). I am most grateful to Père Tabet for supplying me with a copy of these lectures.

36. *Mazmuro* preceding the third reading in the order for the burial of monks.

37. *Mazmuro* preceding the seventh reading in the order for burial of monks.

38. Cyril of Jerusalem, *Catecheses* xxiii, *Myst.* v.21–22 ; Cf. Narsai, *Homily* xvii and Aphraates, *Homily* ix, 10 (R. H. Connolly, *The Liturgical Homilies of Narsai*, Cambridge 1909, *Texts and Studies*, VIII, p.29 and note.)

39. Tabet, pp.39–40.

40. Tabet, pp.60–67.

Chapter 4

1. cf. H. R. Philippeau, 'Textes et rubriques des *Agenda Mortuorum*' in *Archiv fur Liturgiewissenschaft* IV, Regensburg 1955, pp.52–72.

2. M. Andrieu, *Les Ordines Romani du Haut Moyen Age* IV, Louvain 1956, pp.523–530.

3. MS Berlin Phillipps 1667, ff.173^v–174^r. Text printed in H. Frank, 'Der älteste *Ordo defunctorum* der Römischen Liturgie ...', in *Archiv fur Liturgie-wissenschaft*, VII (1962), pp.363–364.

4. For the Cologne MS 123 cf. G. Haenni, 'Un ORDO DEFUNCTORUM du Xe Siècle', in *Ephemerides Liturgicae* LXXIII (1959), pp.431–434.

5. Andrieu, III, p.154. *Ordo* XVI, q. 54; Frank, pp. 369–370.

6. pp.374–375.

7. Dom B. Capelle, 'L'Antienne *In Paradisum*', in *Travaux Liturgiques de doctrine et d'historie* III, Louvain 1967, pp.252ff.

8. Text in H. A. Wilson, *The Gelasian Sacramentary*, Oxford 1894, pp. 295–301.

9. For this theme cf. S. G. F. Brandon, *The Judgment of the Dead* (1967), pp.123–124.

10. Edmund Bishop gives a comparative table of five of the eighth-century texts (Gelasian, Gellone, Godelgaudus of Reims, Rheinau 30, and Alcuin's Supplement) in his *Liturgica Historica*, Oxford 1918, pp.184–189.

11. Bishop, op.cit., p.191 cf. P. de Puniet, *Le Sacramentaire Romain de Gellone*, Rome 1939, p. 316*. Gougaud notes that the invocation of hermits in the prayer first occurs in English rituals of the twelfth century, and that the prayer *Commendo te Omnipotenti Deo*, added in the sixteenth century, was derived from an eleventh-century letter of Peter Damien ('Études sur les *ordines commendationis animae*', in *Ephemerides Liturgicae* NS. IX (1935), p.12).

12. Bishop, p.189.

13. p.168.

14. Philippeau, 'Texts et Rubriques', p.59.

15. For a detailed description, on which the following summary is based, cf. Guy de Valous, *Le Monachisme clunisien des origines au XVe siècle*, Paris 1970, I, pp.294–298. For Cistercian practice see the Cistercian *Consuetudines* XCIII–XCVIII in P. Guignard, *Les Monuments primitifs de la Règle Cistercienne* (Analecta Divionensia), Dijon 1878, pp.204–216.

16. Durandus, *Rationale divinorum officiorum* VII.xxv.35.

17. *Life of St Aelred of Rievaulx* (ed. Powicke), Cap. LVII, p.62.

18. Bede, *Historia Ecclesiastica* iv.23.

19. D. Knowles (ed.), *Lanfranc's Monastic Constitutions* (1951), pp.123–124.

20. Durandus: *Rationale* VII.xxv.39.

21. PL. clxxi.896.

22. Durandus: *Rationale* VII.xxv.43.

23. Cf. A. S. Duncan-Jones, 'The Burial of the Dead,' in W. K. Lowther Clarke (ed.), *Liturgy and Worship* (1932), p. 621.

24. Durandus, *Rationale* VII.xxxv.27, 28.

25. Cf. D. Andrea Cabassut q. in L. Bracaloni: 'Il primo rituale Francescano', *Archivum Franciscum Historicum* XVI (1923), pp.84–85.

26. *Liber Conformitatum*, q. F. J. E. Raby, *Christian Latin Poetry*, Oxford 1953², p.443.

27. The *Dies Irae* was not the only sequence on this theme, as can be seen from another example, Engelbert of Admont's *De Ultimo Iudicio* (fourteenth century), which begins:

Ave, Iesu, tunc pavendus	*Ave Iesu! tunc inferni*
Peccatori metuendus	*Flamma, ignes sempiterni*
Arbiter adveniens.	*Concremabunt perditos!*
In horrenda ignis nube	*Tunc torquebit putens nidor,*
In clangore vocis tubae	*Ignis, frigus, fletus, stridor,*
Orbis totum quatiens!	*Mundi quondam inclytos.*

Text in P. S. Everts, *Hymni Mediaevales*, Zwolle 1950, pp.77–79.

28. For a general account of these developments cf. A. Molinier, *Les Obituaires Français au Moyen Age*, Paris 1890.

29. H. Thurston, *The Memory of our Dead* (1915), pp.43–44. Thurston interprets the three headings mentioned as follows: *Necrologium:* 'primarily the record of the dead of a particular house'; *Liber vitae:* 'a name in which the list of benefactors seems to be the leading idea'; *Martyrologium:* 'probably developed out of the roll of bishops, who formed a class apart in the diptychs, and who were *canonizati*, selected to be commemorated in the Canon of the Mass'.

30. Remiremont Necrology (ninth century), cited Thurston, p.46.

31. In the preface to the *Life of St Cuthbert*, q. Molinier, pp.24–25. Cf. Boniface's request to the abbot of Monte Cassino: 'That there may be between us brotherly charity; that there may be common prayer for the living; that there may be masses celebrated for the dead; that prayers will be said when we mutually exchange the names of our dead ...' (Ibid., p.25).

32. Molinier, p.30.

33. It is thought that the custom may have played some part in the development of the Franciscan and Dominican tertiaries.

34. Molinier (p.40) cites the case of Adalbert, bishop of Augsburg, from the *liber confraternitatem* of St Gall, who, for the privilege of having his anniversary kept with the same honour as the abbots of St Gall, came on pilgrimage, spent a week at the shrine, made frequent visits to the tomb of the saint, entertained the community sumptuously every day and gave offerings to various chapels, &c.

35. Ibid., p.116.

36. Claude Raphine in his *De coniunctione obituum* (beginning of the sixteenth century) considers such problems as: Is it of more advantage to be joined with

the founders and have an annual mass or a daily one? Does a person so united merit the title of founder? Is there a prejudicing of the original obit by the addition of another? Is it licit to unite in this manner the obits of different foundations?

37. q. Thurston, p.114, who also gives the text of a note of the decree made at the Italian abbey of Farfa: 'It was enacted with the consent and at the request of all the older monks of Cluny that as in all the churches of God that are erected throughout the world the festival of All Saints' day is duly kept upon the first day of November, so amongst us on the morrow there should be kept a solemn commemoration of the Faithful departed in the following manner ...'.

38. Thurston, pp.116–117.

39. p.120.

40. S. J. P. van Dijk and J. Hazelden Walker, *The Origins of the Modern Roman Liturgy* (1960), p.341.

41. Text in PL. cxv.1448–1450. Cf. Philippeau, 'Origines et évolution des rites funéraires', *Le Mystère de la Mort et sa Célébration*, Paris 1956, p.204; P.-M. Gy, 'Les Funérailles d'après le rituel de 1614', in *La Maison-Dieu* 44 (1955/iv), pp.70–82.

42. Texts in H. Faehn (ed.), *Manuale Norvegicum (Libri Liturgicae provinciae nidrosiensis medii aevi* I), Oslo 1962, pp.86ff., 94ff.

43. Cf. *Le Mystère de la Mort*, p.203.

Chapter 5

1. B. J. Kidd, *Documents of the Continental Reformation* (1911), pp.227–228.

2. Comparative table in F. E. Brightman, *The English Rite* (1915), I, p.cxxvii.

3. Hermann, *A simple and religious consultation* (1547), 'Of Buriynge'.

4. Ibid.

5. A. L. Richter, *Die Evangelischen Kirchenordnungen des sechzehnten Jahrhunderts*, Weimar 1846, I, p.277.

6. The Norwegian Church Ritual of 1685 provides an even simpler rite: 1. Committal and casting on of earth three times by the minister with an appropriate formula; 2. a psalm whilst others present cast earth on the body; 3. a psalm and a sermon (of not more than one hour) in church. Later Norwegian altar books (1889 and 1920) have, however, provided a more elaborate scheme, with more psalmody, a range of lections, and fuller prayers.

7. Text and commentary in E. E. Yelverton, *The Manual of Olavus Petri, 1529* (1953), pp.49–54, 92–101.

8. Cf. P. Althaus, *The Theology of Martin Luther*, Philadelphia 1966, pp.404–425.

9. The Epistle in the *Missa pro defunctis* in the *Missale Upsalense Nouum*, ed. Yelverton, p.54.

10. J. Dowden, *The Workmanship of the Prayer Book* (1904),[2] p.161.

11. Ibid. pp.161–163.

12. Calvin, *Institutes*, III.xxv.5.

13. Ibid. III.xxv.8.

14. Kidd, p.599.

15. W. D. Maxwell, *John Knox's Genevan Service Book of 1556*, Edinburgh 1931, pp.161, 163–164.

16. W. McMillan, *The Worship of the Scottish Reformed Church, 1550–1638* (1931), p.283.

17. G. W. Sprott (ed.), *Scottish Liturgies of the Reign of King James VI* (1871), p.89.

18. Text in P. Hall, *Reliquiae Liturgicae*, Bath 1847, III, pp.72–73.

19. McMillan, pp.293–295. An ancient pre-Reformation custom was continued in the bell-man going before the cortège.

20. H. Barrow, *A Briefe Discoverie of the False Church*, q. in Horton Davies, *Worship and Theology in England*, I (1534–1603), Princeton & London 1970, pp.333–334.

21. F. Procter & W. H. Frere, *A New History of the Book of Common Prayer* (1901), p.636.

22. p.633n. Brightman, II, pp.873–874; H. A. Wilson, *The Gelasian Sacramentary*, pp.297, 299. For further details cf. Brightman, I, p.cxxviii.

23. Procter & Frere, p.634. Cf. H. C. White, *Tudor Books of Private Devotion*, Wisconsin 1951.

24. M. Bucer, *Scripta Anglicana*, Basle 1577, p.467. In his *Lectures on Ephesians* Bucer comments that in the funeral rites of the primitive churches thanks were given 'that the departed were now in enjoyment of the supreme felicity for which they had hoped. The rest of the ceremony, as we read of it in the ancient doctors, was conducted with godly purity. Our adversaries have translated all the works of godliness into purgatory, of which the older Fathers knew nothing and Augustine was doubtful.' (D. F. Wright (ed.), *Common Places of Martin Bucer*, Appleford 1972, p.227).

25. The phraseology is in fact slightly different from that of the English translation of Hermann, but the substance is exactly the same.

26. It is, nevertheless, primarily a prayer for sharing in the bliss of the resurrection rather than from delivery from the pains of hell. Cf. *The Book of Homilies:* 'Let us think that the soul of man goeth straightway to heaven or else to hell, whereof the one needeth no prayer, and the latter is without redemption.'

27. Strype, *Annals of the Reformation*, Introduction I, iii, 31, *Works*, Oxford 1824, VII, p.44.

28. P. Heylyn, *Ecclesia Restaurata* (1661), ii, p.105.

29. Ibid., p.119.

30. Strype, *Annals* ix; *Works* VII, pp.187–191.

31. Text in *Private Prayers put forth by authority during the Reign of Queen Elizabeth*, Parker Society, Cambridge 1851, pp.57–67. The 1551 Primer allowed the petition that 'light perpetual' might shine upon the departed, but not that God would 'purge them all their sins'. (W. P. Haugaard: *Elizabeth and the English Reformation*, Cambridge 1968, p.14.)

32. Strype, *Annals* ix. loc. cit.; Heylyn, ii, p.119.

33. q. Haugaard, p.115.

34. '& in generali resurrectione, extremo die, nos una cum hoc fratre nostro resuscitati, & receptis corporibus, regnemus una tecum in vita aeterna.'

35. Haugaard, pp.115 and n., 124.

36. p.124.

37. p.164.

38. pp.226–227.

39. J. F. H. New, *Anglican and Puritan* (1964), p.42.

40. S. B. Babbage, *Puritanism and Richard Bancroft* (1962), p.155.

41. E. Cardwell, *A History of Conferences and other proceedings connected with the Revision of the Book of Common Prayer*, Oxford 1841, pp.332–333. The objection concerning the 'sure and certain hope' is similar to that made by the Committee of Divines appointed by the House of Lords in 1641, cf. Cardwell, p.277.

42. Cardwell, pp.361–362.

43. Hall, *Reliquiae Liturgicae*, IV, pp.103–105.

44. J. H. Blunt, *The Annotated Book of Common Prayer* (1876), p.301.

45. T. J. Fawcett, *The Liturgy of Comprehension, 1689* (1973), pp. 147–149.

46. A. E. Peaston, *The Prayer Book Tradition in the Free Churches* (1964), p.49.

47. Horton Davies, IV, p.258.

48. Cf. P. T. Marsh, *The Victorian Church in Decline* (1969), pp. 251–263; Owen Chadwick, *The Victorian Church* II (1970), pp.202–207.

49. Horton Davies, IV, pp.96, 106n., 108f.

50. Peaston, pp.57–58, 85.

51. C. P. Gould & J. H. Shakespeare, *A Manual for Free-Church Ministers* (1905), pp.19–31.

52. pp.40–51.

53. A. E. Peaston, *The Prayer Book Revisions of the Victorian Evangelicals*, Dublin 1963, p.24.

54. *The Ecclesiologists* XIV (1855), pp.97–99.

55. H. B. Swete, *Services and Service-books before the Reformation*, p.171n.

56. T. W. Belcher, *Robert Brett, his life and work* (1889), pp.173–174.

57. For further details of nineteenth-century practice, cf. Geoffrey Rowell, 'Nineteenth-century attitudes and practices', in G. Cope (ed.), *Dying, Death and Disposal* (1970).

Chapter 6

1. The various arguments on this subject are clearly set out in an Anglican context in *Prayer and the Departed* (A Report of the Archbishops' Commission on Christian Doctrine), 1971.

2. Text in *The New Funeral Mass Book*, Redemptorist Publications, Chawton 1971.

3. Cf. T. Stone and A. Cunningham, 'The Chicago Experimental Funeral Rite', *Concilium* II, No.4 (1968), pp.49–52.

4. W. Jardine Grisbrooke, 'Towards a Liturgy of Committal', in G. Cope, *Dying, Death and Disposal*, 1970, p.61. The whole of this article is a good examination of what a Christian burial rite should express.

5. The Church of England Liturgical Commission, *Alternative Services: Second Series* (1965), pp.105–106.

6. *The Proposed Book of Common Prayer and Other Rites and Ceremonies of the Church*, New York 1977, p.50.

7. Ibid., pp.480–481.

8. Ibid., p.497.

9. Ibid., p.500.

10. For Victorian mourning customs cf. J. Morley, *Death, Heaven and the Victorians* (1971), pp. 19–31, 63–79.

11. E. Jackson, *The Christian Funeral: its meaning, its purpose, and its modern practice*, New York 1966, pp.24, 25.

12. J. Hick, *Death and Eternal life* (1976), p.85.
13. L. Pincus, *Death and the Family: the importance of mourning* (1976), p.203.
14. p.45.
15. p.254.
16. A. MacIntyre, *Secularization and Moral Change* (1967), pp.69–70.
17. H. J. M. Nouwens, *Creative Ministry*, New York 1971, pp.91–92.
18. Morley, pp.41–51.
19. pp.91ff.
20. Cf. Cope, op.cit., p.80.
21. pp.85–98.

Select bibliography

(The place of publication of books is London unless otherwise stated.)

ANDRIEU, M., *Les Ordines Romani du Haut Moyen Age* (Spicilegium Sacrum Lovaniense), Louvain 1956.

AZZI, J., 'Offices des funérailles et théologie de la mort d'après le manuscript Vat. Syr. 59', *Proche-Orient Chrétien* XXIII (1973).

BABBAGE, S. B., *Puritanism and Richard Bancroft* (1962).

BADGER, G. P., *The Nestorians and their Rituals*, 2 vols. (1852).

BELCHER, T. W., *Robert Brett, of Stoke Newington, his life and work* (1889).

BENDER, A. P., 'Beliefs, rites and customs of the Jews connected with death, burial and mourning', *Jewish Quarterly Review* VII (1894–1895).

BISHOP, E., *Liturgica Historica*, Oxford 1918.

BLOOMFIELD, M. W., *The Seven Deadly Sins*, Michigan 1952.

BLUNT, J. H., *The Annotated Book of Common Prayer* (1876).

BRACALONI, L., 'Il primo rituale Francescano', *Archivum Franciscum Historicum* XVI (1923).

BRANDON, S. G. F., *The Judgement of the Dead* (1967).

BRIGHTMAN, F. E., *The English Rite*, 2 vols. (1915).

BRIGHTMAN, F. E. *Liturgies Eastern and Western* I, Oxford 1896.

BURMESTER, O. H. E. KHS-, *The Egyptian or Coptic Church, a detailed description of her Liturgical Services and the rites and ceremonies observed in the administration of her sacraments* (Publications de la Société d'archéologie copte), Cairo 1967.

BUDGE, E. A. WALLIS, *The Bandlet of Righteousness: an Ethiopian Book of the Dead* (1929).

CAPELLE, B., 'L' Antienne IN PARADISUM', *Travaux Liturgiques de doctrine et d'histoire* III, Louvain 1967.

CARDWELL, E., *A History of Conferences and other proceedings connected with the revision of the Book of Common Prayer*, Oxford 1841.

CENTRE DE PASTORALE LITURGIQUE, *Le Mystère de la Mort et sa Célébration* (Lex Orandi XII), Paris 1956.

CONNOLLY, R. H., *The Liturgical Homilies of Narsai* (Texts & Studies VII), Cambridge 1909.

CONNOLLY, R. H. *Didascalia Apostolorum*, Oxford 1929.

CONYBEARE, F. C. and MACLEAN, A. J., *Rituale Armenorum*, Oxford 1905.

COPE, G. (ed.), *Dying, Death and Disposal* (1970).

COQUIN, R-G., *Les Canons d'Hippolyte* (Patrologia Orientalis XXI), Paris 1966.

COWLEY, R., 'Parish Life in the Ethiopian Countryside', *Sobornost*, V. 3 (1966).

COWLEY, R, 'Attitudes to the Dead in the Ethiopian Orthodox Church', *Sobornost* VI, 4 (1972).

CUMONT, F., *After Life in Roman Paganism* (1922).

DANIÉLOU, J., *Les Anges et leur Mission d'après les Pères de l'Église* (Collection Irénikon NS. 5), Gembloux 1952.

DANIÉLOU, J., *The Theology of Jewish Christianity* (A History of Early Christian Doctrine I), (1964).

DAVIES, HORTON, *Worship and Theology in England* I (1970).

DIJK, S. J. P. van, and HAZLEDEN WALKER, J., *The Origins of the Modern Roman Liturgy* (1960).

DOWDEN, J., *The Workmanship of the Prayer Book* (1904)[2].

DYGGVE, E., *History of Salonitan Christianity*, Oslo 1951.

EVERTS, P. S., *Hymni Mediaevales*, Zwolle 1950.

EUCHOLOGION TO MEGA (in Greek), Venice 1869.

FAEHN, H. (ed.), *Manuale Norvegicum* (Libri Liturgicae provinciae nidrosiensis medii aevi I), Oslo 1962.

FRANK, H., 'Die älteste Ordo Defunctorum der Römischen Liturgie,' *Archiv fur Liturgie-Wissenschaft* VII (1962).

FREISTEDT, E., *Altchristliche Totengedächtnistage und Beziehung zum Jenseits- glauben und Totenkulten der Antike*, Münster 1928.

GOUGAUD, L., 'Études sur les *ordines commendationis animae*', *Ephemerides Liturgicae* NS. IX (1935).

GOULD, C. P. and SHAKESPEARE, J. H., *A Manual for Free-Church Ministers* (1905).

GRABKA, G., 'Christian Viaticum: a study of its cultural background', *Traditio*, IX (1953).

GUIGNARD, P., *Les Monuments primitifs de la Règle Cistercienne* (Analecta Divionensia), Dijon 1878.

GY, P-M., 'Les Funérailles d'après le rituel 1614', *La Maison-Dieu* XLIV (1955).

HAENNI, G., 'Un ORDO DEFUNCTORUM du Xe Siècle', *Ephemerides Liturgicae* LXXIII (1959).

HALL, I. H., 'The Nestorian Ritual of Washing the Dead', *Hebraica* IV (1882).

HALL, P., *Reliquiae Liturgicae*, Bath 1847.

HAMMERSCHMIDT, E., *Studies in the Ethiopic Anaphoras*, Berlin 1961.

HAPGOOD, I. F., *Service Book of the Holy Orthodox-Catholic Apostolic (Greco-Russian) Church*, New York 1906.

HARDEN, J. M., *The Ethiopic Didascalia* (1920).

HARDEN, J. M., *An Introduction to Ethiopic Christian Literature* (1926).

HARDEN, J. M., *The Anaphoras of the Ethiopic Liturgy* (1928).

HAUGAARD, W. P., *Elizabeth and the English Reformation*, Cambridge 1968.

HENNECKE, E., *New Testament Apocrypha*, 2 vols. (1963–1965).

HERTZ, J. H., *The Authorised Daily Prayer Book with Commentary* (1947).

HICK, J., *Death and Eternal Life* (1976).

IDELSOHN, A. Z., *Jewish Liturgy and its developments*, New York 1932.

JACKSON, E., *The Christian Funeral*, New York 1966.

JEREMIAS, J., *New Testament Theology*, I (1971)

JUNGMANN, J. A., *The Early Liturgy* (1958).

KIDD, B. J., *Documents of the Continental Reformation* (1911).

KNOWLES, M. D., *Lanfranc's Monastic Constitutions* (1951).

LOWTHER CLARKE, W. K. (ed.), *Liturgy and Worship* (1932).

MACINTYRE, A., *Secularization and Moral Change* (1967).

MACOMBER, W., 'The Funeral Liturgy of the Chaldean Church', *Concilium* II (1968).

MAGISTRETTI, M., *Manuale Ambrosianum*, Milan 1905.

MARTIMORT, A. G. (ed.), *L'Église en Prière*, Tournai 1965³.

MAXWELL, W. D., *John Knox's Genevan Service Book of 1556*, Edinburgh, 1931.

McMILLAN, W., *The Worship of the Scottish Reformed Church, 1550–1638* (1931).

MOLINIER, A., *Les Obituaires Français au Moyen Age*, Paris 1890.

MORLEY, J., *Death, Heaven and the Victorians* (1971).

New Funeral Mass Book (Redemptorist Publications), Chawton 1971.

NEW, J. F. H., *Anglican and Puritan* (1964).

O'CONNOR, M. C., *The Art of Dying Well*, New York 1942.

PATCH, H. R., *The Other World according to descriptions in medieval literature*, Cambridge, Mass. 1950.

PEASTON, A. E., *The Prayer Book Revisions of the Victorian Evangelicals*, Dublin 1963.

PEASTON, A. E., *The Prayer Book Tradition in the Free Churches* (1964).

PHILLIPPEAU, H. R., 'Textes et rubriques des *Agenda Mortuorum*', *Archiv fur Liturgiewissenschaft* IV (1955).

PINCUS, L., *Death and the Family* (1976).

Private Prayers put forward by authority during the Reign of Queen Elizabeth (Parker Society), Cambridge 1851.

PROCTER, F., and FRERE, W. H., *A New History of the Book of Common Prayer* (1901).

PUNIET, P. de, *La Sacramentaire Romain de Gellone*, Rome 1939.

QUASTEN, J., '*Vetus superstitio et nova religio:* the problem of *Refrigerium* in the ancient church of North Africa', *Harvard Theological Review* XXIII (1940).

QUASTEN, J. 'Der Gute Hirte in Frühchristlicher Totenliturgie und Grabeskunst', *Miscellanea Giovanni Mercati* (Studi e Testi, CXXI), Vatican 1941.

RABY, F. J. E., *Christian Latin Poetry*, Oxford 1953².

RAHNER, H., *Greek Myths and Christian Mystery* (1963).

RICHTER, A. L., *Die Evangelischen Kirchenordnungen des sechzehnten Jahrhunderts*, Weimar 1846.

RIVIÈRE, J., 'Rôle du démon au jugement particulier chez les Pères', *Revue des sciences religieuses* IV (1924).

RUSH, A. C., 'The colors of black and red in the liturgy of the dead', in P. Granfield and J. A. Jungmann (eds.), *Kyriakon: Festschrift Johannes Quasten*, Münster 1970.

RUTLEDGE, D., *Cosmic Theology: the Ecclesiastical Hierarchy of Pseudo-Denys, an Introduction* (1964).

SPROTT, G. W. (ed.), *Scottish Liturgies of the Reign of James VI* (1871).

STONE, R. & CUNNINGHAM, A., 'The Chicago Experimental Funeral Rite', *Concilium* II (1968).

STRYPE, J., *Annals of the Reformation* (*Works*, VII), Oxford 1824.

THURSTON, H., *The Memory of our Dead* (1915).

TOYNBEE, J. M. C., *Death and Burial in the Roman World* (1971).

VALOUS, G. de., *Le Monachisme clunisien des origines au XVe siècle*, Paris 1970.

WHITE, H. C., *Tudor Books of Private Devotion*, Wisconsin 1951.

WILSON, H. A., *The Gelasian Sacramentary*, Oxford 1894.

WOOLLEY, R. M., *Coptic Offices* (1930).

WORDSWORTH, J., *Bishop Sarapion's Prayer Book* (1910)[2].

YELVERTON, E. E., *The Manual of Olavus Petri, 1529* (1953).

Index of scriptural passages

(excluding Psalms)

(References in heavy type indicate passages used as lessons)

Index of liturgical texts

General index